101 Days for a More Mindful Hiring Method

POWER
HIRE

101 Days for a More Mindful Hiring Method

POWER HIRE

BETH SMITH

Power Hire: 101 Days for a More Mindful Hiring Method

Copyright ©2023 by Beth Smith, A-list Interviews.

Softcover ISBN: 978-1-950880-10-2
eBook ISBN: 978-1-950880-12-6

Book design by AuthorSourceMedia.
Printed by AuthorSourceMedia LLC in the United States of America.
https://www.AuthorSourceMedia.com
https://a-listinterviews.com/

DEDICATION

For Katy: who makes me laugh harder than anyone I have ever met. Thanks for singing "Dear John" at the top of your lungs all this summer. I am sure that it will be a blog in my book one day. Love you baby girl!

For My Great Aunt Ruthie Leiper: She died on Thanksgiving Day 1988. Her estate settled about 20 years later, and I received a $6,000.00 check that kept me in business during the recession. Since then, I have felt her having my back through some really hard times.

INTRODUCTION

101 Days to a More Mindful Hiring Method!

Several weeks ago, I was having dinner with my brother, Alex, and I told him that I was writing my third book.

"How do you come up with more things to write?" he asked.

"Everywhere I look, I find a situation that I can turn into a hiring example. It is a mindset," I said.

That is how hiring is: It is a mindset. You have to stay in the hiring mindset in order to hire a top-notch employee, and that is why I wrote my third book, *POWER HIRE! 101 Days to a More Mindful Hiring Method*. It is designed to be read cover to cover, either in order, or you can simply open up the book and read whatever page you land on. That will be the message that you need to hear. (You can also read *Why Can't I Hire Good People?* for a step-by step guide in hiring, and *Hire Power* for more tips and insights.)

This book will give you daily reminders that will keep you mindful of your next great hire. The tips and insights will remind you to:

- Keep the bigger picture in mind, the long-term success of your company.

- Remember that the perfect hire is waiting to be hired.

- Stay open minded during your interviewing process.

- Remember you are hiring people, not perfection.

- Consider individuals that you may not normally hire.

- Remember that settling for "less than" can mean problems down the road.

- Consider how a potential hire fits your company culture.

- Remember that the way forward when hiring may look like a never-ending road, there is an end to that road.

Whether you are a CEO, an HR Director for a multi-national corporation, or a sole proprietor looking to expand your business, the skills you will learn by reading this book will definitely upgrade your hiring, training, and retention success rate! When you're ready, A-list Interviews Inc. can help you design and implement the hiring process you need. In the meantime, this book will give you tips and insights that will help you understand *who* you want to hire and *why*.

Happy Hiring!

Beth Smith

Day 1:
Diet, Exercise, Fire Someone

As each New Year begins, many of us take the opportunity to re-group and redefine goals for our businesses. This time is often filled with renewed energy to get our lives and work in order. As a part of your New Year's goals, it might also be time to fire that one employee who is not contributing to your company's vision.

The impact of an unengaged employee on your business can be catastrophic. Decreased productivity, lowered company morale, and miserable working environments have been common complaints by my clients, as they make the decision to part ways with an employee. I say, "Start the New Year fresh!"

A past client of mine had an employee who consistently gave her ultimatums. The threats were often, "If you don't do this, then I will quit." Who wants to work with an individual who is constantly threatening you? The team was struggling to work with the individual, my client was unhappy with the performance of the individual, yet the concept of firing and replacing this person seemed daunting and ill-timed. When my client finally became fed up, they did indeed fire the employee. I won't sugar coat the transition. It was hard, uncomfortable and came at a terrible time, but my client knew this was the right decision for the company.

In addition, the busiest day of the year for applicants looking for a job is the second Tuesday in January. Think about this: The people who are fed up with their work environments are also looking to make a change. If you want to start the New Year with someone who *really* wants to work for you, get going! Now is the time.

Power Thought

New Year, new goals,
new awesome employee ... and new culture!

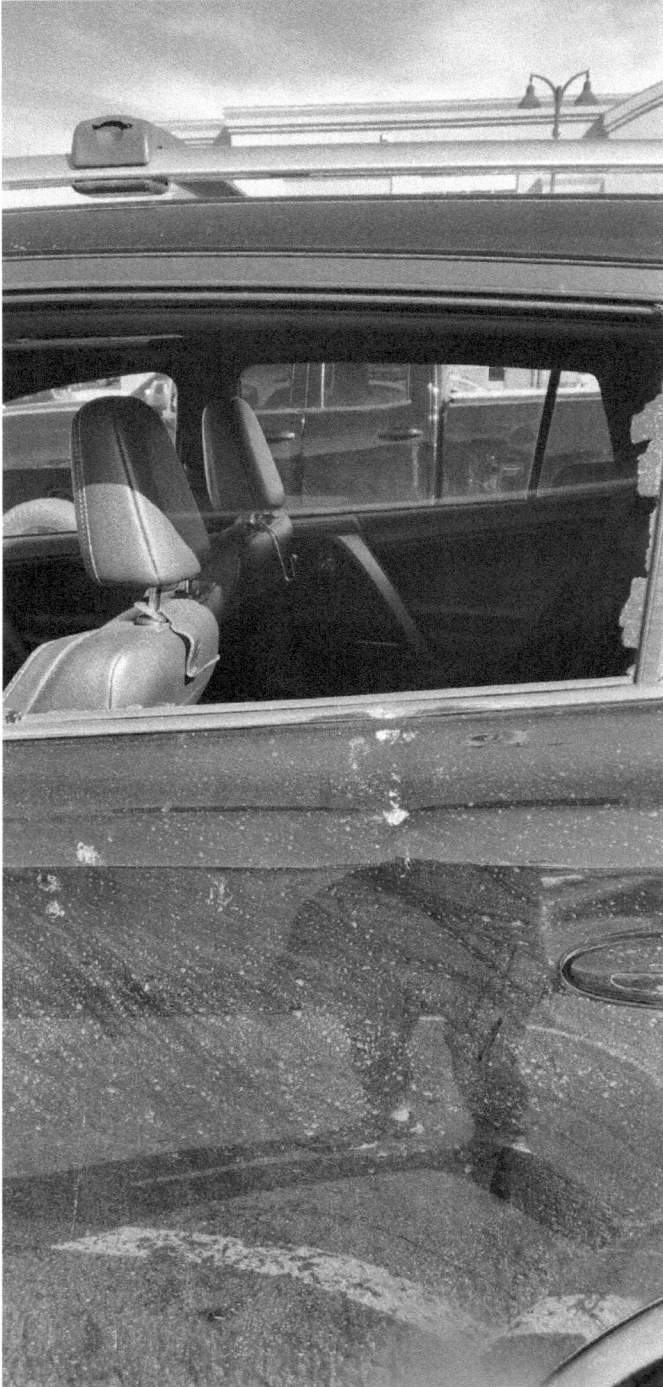

Day 2:
My Stolen Wallet

One day last spring, I bee-bopped into the gym on a beautiful Saturday morning. After completing my stretches, I climbed on a stationary bike for a long ride. A few minutes later, one of the boys who works the front desk came over to me and said, "Do you drive a black Toyota Rav 4?"

"Yes!" I replied. Why are you asking?"

"Well ma'am, it was broken into."

Horrified, I ran out to my car, only to see no window on the driver's side rear door and glass everywhere, and my wallet was gone.

I spent the rest of the day calling credit card companies and canceling cards, when suddenly it occurred to me: I was supposed to be on a plane to Canada first thing Monday morning. I couldn't drive my car with a missing window, because it was snowing. I couldn't order an Uber, because I didn't have a credit card. I couldn't ride the bus, because I had no way to get to the bus stop. While I had my passport and a little bit of cash, what would happen if I had an emergency in a foreign country?

It was time to rally the troops.

I called my client in Canada, and he graciously pre-paid all of my expenses. My neighbor kindly offered to drive me to the airport *and* pick me up. A woman from the gym, who I barely know, wanted to provide me with cash and her credit card. I didn't take her up on that offer, but what an amazing gesture! Several of my friends gave me food, money, and shared their experiences with their own stolen credit cards, gave hugs, and offered listening ears. People from the gym extended their support through kind words and sympathy for my situation. Even the police gave advice on what things to watch out for in the future.

While having my wallet stolen was a terrible experience that cost me a lot of money and time, I am overwhelmed with the love and support that I received. The outpouring of kindness that came my way gave me an extra bounce in my step. And the life lesson that I learned was that even when things look awful, you can find something good. Focus on the miracles, not the lack.

Power Thought

You always have the choice to look at
a *set-back* as a chance to *re-set*.

Day 3:
When You Are Tired of Interviewing –
Part 1

My daughter, Katy, is about to graduate from college. She is also in job search hell. Thirty-seven job applications in nine different states. She's heard back from twenty-five, interviewed at seventeen, and has had two "No's." She has had six job offers, but five of them aren't in the department that she wants and one is in a terrible part of town. Keep in mind that this is on top of full-time school work, two clinicals and a part time job. When we talked recently, she said, "Mom, I'm tired. And not the kind of tired where I need to go to bed early, but *life-tired*."

■ ■ ■ ■ ■

My clients totally get the concept of *life-tired*. The numbers from the last search/hire that we completed in eight weeks looked like this:

Total applicants: 260
First interviews: 36
Second interviews: 7
Third interviews: 2

It is easy to see why everyone on both sides of the table is life-tired.

■ ■ ■ ■ ■

Last week, Katy flew to Texas for an in-person interview that knocked her socks off. The synergy from that interview completely changed her energy, her perspective, and her excitement about her future. "Mom," she said, "I am no longer worried about finding the right job. I don't even have a job offer yet, but I know the right one is coming. I just *feel* it."

"Are you still feeling life-tired?" I asked.

"Oh no. I am life-excited!"

■ ■ ■ ■ ■

One interview can change your entire life, regardless of the outcome. One candidate/employer can transform you from life-tired, to life-excited. Put one foot in front of the other and keep moving forward. Your person/job is on its way!

Power Thought

The middle of your search is the hardest part, and it is so easy to settle! *Don't!* Stay focused through life-tired in order to get to life-excited!

Day 4:
When You Are Tired of Interviewing –
Part 2

In Part 1 of this blog, I wrote about my daughter's frustrating job search. Out of thirty-seven jobs that Katy applied for, she heard back from about half. She also received a job offer from a hospital that she didn't even interview with (a mistake), and was offered a job on the spot, but then was subsequently rejected by email. Three days later, she was offered five jobs in departments that she didn't want, and she broke down crying, stating that she was going to be living in my basement for the rest of her life!

Shortly thereafter, she received a call from a nursing manager at a hospital in Dallas. They had about a six-minute conversation, then the woman said, "We are having in-person interviews in Dallas next week."

Katy replied, "Well, I am going to school in Miami."

The woman said they could do a zoom call.

Katy decided to fly to Dallas for the interview, because it was a job she really wanted. The woman promised to send Katy an email with all the details ... but Katy never received that email. She called the woman several times but didn't hear back. She finally called the HR department to get the address of the hospital and find out where to go for the interview. She arrived at the right hospital on time, and had a *fantastic* interview. Katy was so excited!

The following Friday, Katy received an email at 8 p.m. from the nursing manager stating how sorry she was. She had been sending emails to the wrong email address for Katy, and realized that Katy had never received any of her communication. Six days later, Katy received her job offer. She was ecstatic!

The lesson here is that you can't mess up the right thing. It is mind-boggling to think about all the ways this could have been a disaster, but it wasn't.

When you are tired of interviewing, keep plugging away. Your right job/employee/opportunity will present itself in time, and you can't mess it up. Go for it!

Power Thought

You can't mess up the right thing,
and the wrong thing will always be a struggle.

Day 5:
My New Best Friend, Stephanie

For several days in a row, at 3:02 p.m., always from different numbers, I got a call from someone named Stephanie. In her sing-songy voice, she cheerily asks me about my day. She always sounded happy and content, while pitching questions about how she might be able to help me with a business loan and/or my car warranty. I finally clued in that she was a robot, but to be fair to Artificial Intelligence, it took me a while.

Artificial Intelligence is alive and well, and now, with Stephanie's help, robots will be conducting interviews on behalf of both candidates and companies. According an article in the Denver Business Journal, what will become even more important will be the ability to conduct effective interviews and reference checks.[1]

Are you curious about how Stephanie is going to affect your business? I highly recommend attending an AI conference hosted by Sam Reeve, founder of the Comp Team, or any other AI conference that you can find.[2] AI experts can help you navigate how these rapid changes will affect your business, and then you too can put Stephanie in her place.

Power Thought
Best friends should be human, not robots.

---

1   https://www.bizjournals.com/bizwomen/news/latest-news/2023/02/chatgpt-job-interview-best-practices.html?page=all
2   https://aicompadvantage.com/register

9

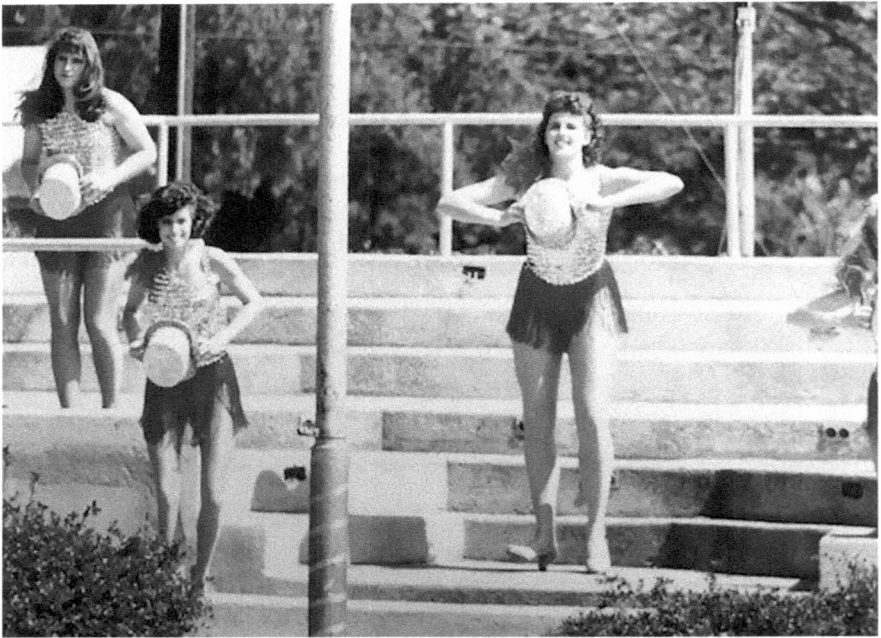

Day 6:
When You Learn a New Skill

When I was a little girl, I used to play at Cherry Park. There was a bandstand in this park, and I spent hours on that bandstand pretending to be in front of an audience. I started off dancing on that bandstand (**see photo above**), but I knew that one day, I would be a public speaker. I had no idea what I was going to say in front of my audiences, but that didn't stop me from believing that one day I would speak in front of people all over the world.

Many moons later, I have met that goal, and I continue to speak in front of groups on a regular basis. I love my work! However, I also miss working with my individual companies and clients. I miss the camaraderie. I miss getting to know the teams of people, and seeing where and how they work. I miss watching the dynamics play out. And I really miss watching my clients have "light bulb" moments in their searches.

Don't get me wrong; I'm so glad that I learned how to present in front of groups of people. I am so proud of myself for graduating from Mikki Williams' Speaker School and working hard to be a professional speaker. And, I am especially glad to be able to offer a training service to my clients. I think that public speaking has made me a better consultant.

Learning a new skill makes your employees more versatile and well-rounded, which is why you *must* invest in professionally developing your people. The benefits of professional development go way beyond what you think it might, including boosting your employee's confidence and making them more willing to contribute. Developing ancillary skills will greatly help your employee with their everyday job while giving them self-assuredness to branch out in other areas. A definite win-win!

Yes, I am still on the bandstand. I am also behind the scenes supporting the bandstand moments for others. How can I help support yours?

Power Thought

Support your employees' bandstand dreams,
because in turn, they will help support yours.

Day 7:
The Chrysler LeBaron Convertible

When I was in college a gazillion years ago, I had a great friend, Beth Bratton. We were connected at the hip and two peas in a pod. Beth was head cheerleader at her huge Dallas high school, great GPA and cute, darling, and precious. In my opinion, she was the total package.

When Beth started looking at colleges, her father told her that whatever money she received from scholarships, he would put that amount of money towards a new car. Beth immediately responded with, "Game. On!" She applied to every scholarship that she could get her hands on and had several formal interviews, but she was rejected time after time after time.

Beth was super frustrated, because she had her eye on this hot Chrysler LeBaron convertible. She was determined to be driving that car around Austin!

Finally, Beth had an interview with Wells Fargo. She just knew that she wouldn't get the scholarship, because she hadn't received any of the others. She just didn't care anymore. She made peace with the fact that she wouldn't get the car, and she walked into that interview and nailed it. The bank gave her a $50k scholarship, and she promptly purchased her dream car. We drove all over Austin in that car, and in one particularly memorable trip, we drove to South Padre for spring break. (That's all I will say about that trip. ☺)

What does this have to do with hiring? Just about the time that you are ready to give up, your dream job or dream employee will show up. When you are so frustrated that you don't care anymore, you're offered the perfect job, or your ideal candidate walks in your door. When you are sick and tired of waiting, your wildest dreams come true.

It is called letting go. And it is the hardest part of your search.

What I tell my clients is that when they are tired of working with me, their amazing employee will walk through their door, and all their hard work will have been worth it. And when they do, they will have more time to take off driving down the highway in their dream car.

Power Thought

Dream of yourself in a convertible with the top down
and not a care in the world. Hold out until you get it.

Day 8:
Crabs or Turtles

If you've ever watched YouTube videos, you might have seen one about a bunch of crabs in a bucket. The crabs scramble to get out by crawling on top of each other to get to the top. Fascinating enough, once one crab gets to the top, the other crabs pull it back in! The group keeps all members in the bucket, instead of focusing on getting out. Instead of improving their surroundings, the group of crabs keep all others stuck in the muck.

Turtles, on the other hand ... If there is a turtle who has somehow turned over onto its back, and is scrambling to turn back over, other turtles will rush to its rescue. As a group, they will help that turtle turn back over and land on its feet. The success of one equals the success of all.

■   ■   ■   ■   ■

If you want to create a thriving, synergistic, and productive culture in your organization, you must fire the crabs and find more turtles. No one gets to the top without a lot of help and support, and getting to the next level isn't easy. Having just one crab on your team can make the difference between success and failure.

Power Thought

Ask yourself, *Does your company culture revolve around turtles or crabs?*

Day 9:
Take Your Headphones O-F-F!

I was having dinner with a friend, and we were discussing how hard it was to meet new people. I then turned to my friend and said, "It's funny; I spend five-to-seven hours a week in the gym, and I don't know anyone there."

Alarmed, she asked, "Why?"

"I think it's because I wear headphones."

"Well, take those headphones off!" she replied.

■ ■ ■ ■ ■

Take your headphones off. What a concept!

This also applies to recruiting. We put up so many roadblocks for applicants to even apply for a job, and then complain that our applicant pool is so low. We keep doing what we've always done and expect different results. This is the definition of insanity!

Take your headphones off and look at your application process from a potential candidate's point of view. Do they have to retype their whole resume into your applicant tracking system? Do they have to copy and paste their references in three different places? Are you making them jump through near-impossible hoops to even be considered for the job? Are you using Artificial Intelligence to interview your candidates? Are your candidates not even talking to a real person for weeks in the hiring process?

If you want to change the quality of your candidates, maybe it is time for an audit of your hiring process. Take your headphones off and encourage people to talk to y-o-u.

■ ■ ■ ■ ■

I am so happy to report that I've made some really great friends and connections at the gym, simply because I allowed myself to be available.

Power Thought

Take off your headphones and open the door to new opportunities. You never know who you might meet!

Day 10:
Flag Your Candidates

When I bought my house several years ago, I hung a Texas Longhorn flag over my garage. It has become a marker!

My friend, Meryem, came over one Sunday and said, "Your flag needs to be re-hung."

"It was torn by the wind. I need to order a new one," I responded.

"Well, whatever you do, don't get rid of it; that flag is how I know your house!"

She isn't the only friend to tell me this.

■   ■   ■   ■   ■

What does my Longhorn flag have to do with hiring and recruiting?

As a business leader, it is your job to lead your candidates through the hiring process with signposts. Your process should be *clearly* marked, so your candidates know where they are and where they are headed. In other words, don't make your candidates jump through so many hoops that they get lost. Your ad should be short, sweet, and to the point. Your website should have a button that says, "Apply here." Your applicant tracking system (ATS) shouldn't make your candidate input all of the data that is written on their resume. It should *never* take a candidate *hours* to apply. They will get frustrated, and rightly so. During the interview, tell them when they will have answers from you and meet that deadline.

Lead your potential candidates through the process with a clearly marked trail. They will be so grateful, and you will have your pick of great staff.

Power Thought
Flag great candidates with a clearly
marked hiring process.

Day 11:
The "R" Word

For the past several weeks, I've had a really cranky client. When he snapped at an employee in front of me, I followed him into his office to gently confront him.

"What is going on with you?" I asked him.

After a while, he finally confessed to me the issue: "I am afraid of the recession."

■　■　■　■　■

Who can blame him? Whenever there is a looming recession, every news outlet hits us over the head for weeks, and freaks people out. No wonder people panic!

So, let's shift the conversation by changing the "r" word to something more proactive ... like "re-set" or "re-fresh." What a slow-down in business does is give business owners a minute to "re-organize" and "re-direct." Let's be proactive, not reactive! Here are three tips:

1. Perform an audit of your current staff. Who is great? Who needs more training? Who needs to go?

2. Look at your processes for sales, inventory, and production. Where are the holes? Where are the issues? What are your clients reporting?

3. Finally, look at your leadership style. Are you negative? Are you snapping at employees? If so, you may also need a re-set.

Whatever you are going through, you can do this. I've got your back.

Power Thought
The "r" word doesn't have to be repulsive.
It can be rejuvenating!

Day 12:
Mow Your Lawn

As most of you know, I am a *diehard* University of Texas Longhorn fan. I am such a fan that my Oklahoma-loving neighbor and I have agreed that we just won't speak to each other from September 1st to December 1st. We have a very amicable relationship for the other nine months of the year.

When the Longhorns played Kansas, several of the Texas players were interviewed, along with the coach Steve Sarkisian, and the mantra was to "Mow Your Lawn." Each player had a different description to what that phrase meant, because they all have a different job to do on the field. Each player is responsible for their part of the field, and without every individual doing their part, the team won't perform well.

I have so much respect for this type of leadership!

Each person on the team knows what their job is, and most importantly, how their job connects to the overall team success. *And* they know all of this with a three-word phrase: Mow your lawn.

■　■　■　■　■

I am happy to say that Texas beat Kansas. After year two, Steve Sarkisian ended the season with an 8–5 record. Better than last year, and with this type of leadership, I have lots of hope for our future seasons.

Power Thought

Mow your lawn. And, "Hook 'em Horns!"

Day 13:
Do You Hear What I Hear?

Over the Thanksgiving holiday a few years ago, my daughter and I were listening to the radio. A Zac Brown Band song came on that we both love. I began belting out the tune at the top of my lungs and sang along to the chorus of "Long Gone" in perfect pitch—to me, at least. Katy laughed uproariously. "Mom", she yelled, "Those aren't the words!"

"Yes, they are!"

She giggled, then said "No, really. It's not 'Long Gone'. It's 'Home Grown'!"

She had to Google it for me to believe her.

■　　■　　■　　■　　■

This misunderstanding happens in interviews for new employees all the time. Someone on the interview team will recount what the candidate said, and someone else will have heard the words from the person completely differently. The very first step in the analysis of an interview for the hiring team is to agree to what the candidate actually *said*. The candidate's choice of words is very important.

For example, "My boss is really great to work with." Did they really say "with"? Are you sure they didn't say "My boss is really great to work *for*"? That simple word changes the entire meaning of the sentence, as well as the intent of the comment. The word "with" denotes that the candidate doesn't acknowledge their bosses' authority, and if they don't acknowledge it in the interview, they really won't when they have direct deposit.

I talk about listening to the exact words all the time to my clients to ensure they hire someone who will truly fit with the company culture, leadership style, and even the position itself. If you are not paying attention, you can miss something important in an interview, which can lead to a bad hire.

You can also embarrass yourself in front of your beloved daughter.

Power Thought

Did you really hear what you thought you heard?

Day 14:
Quiet Quitting is QUITE the Trend

I have a client who is really worried about "quiet quitting," and he called me to discuss his concerns.

"Do you know what quiet quitting is?" I asked.

"Yes! It's when employees quit working but are still on your payroll!"

It's easy to see why he is worried.

Quiet quitting is a very confusing term, because it doesn't involve employees actually *leaving* the company. According to an article on LinkedIn, a more accurate term is "acting your wage" or doing nothing more than your job.[1]

I really hate terms like this, because it makes my clients super nervous. When the business leader in an organization is nervous, then everyone on the staff follows suit. And that makes quiet quitting a self-fulling prophecy.

Instead of fearing this trend, let's re-frame it: What if quiet quitting is simply employees having better boundaries around work? What if employees stop killing themselves at work, and engage in more self-care? What if, instead of focusing on "quitting," we focused on training and retention?

At the end of the day, whatever term you use, it is important to focus on being proactive and not reactive. When you are a proactive leader, you are calmer, and that feeling eases any tension for your staff.

Power Thought

Quiet quitting is quite the trend.
Just maybe not the trend that you thought.

---

1   https://www.linkedin.com/business/talent/blog/talent-engagement/why-we-cant-quit-talking-about-quiet-quitting?TRK=orgsocial-quiet-quitting-facebook-9-14-22&fbclid=IwAR2a7LCyRaP_NcRBDXBDifLGpCJJgVSnWN0_t4QnmlHD7sUHVzj3Pz6popA

Day 15:
Zombies in the Workplace

Halloween has been hit-and-miss in the workplace, in my experience. Some companies really promote it by buying pounds of candy and giving out prizes for the best costumes. Other companies don't celebrate, with the mindset of, "Please don't bring candy here! I am trying so hard to stick to my diet!"

But this year, there is something in the air. The fall is so beautiful, the air is calm, and winter is late to the party. Most of my clients are in the mood to do something different … like celebrate.

Here are a couple of the comments that I have heard from my clients:

- "I started buying chocolate mid-September. I never do that!"

- "This year, by God, I am dressing up for Halloween. I haven't done that in a decade."

We have all been walking around in a COVID-Zombie fog the last couple years. In many countries, Halloween is the beginning of the New Year, and it definitely feels that way now. We are all tired of walking around half-dead in a zombie state and looking ghostly.

I encourage you to step out of the norm. Make the effort to celebrate in a way that you haven't done in a long time. Buy the candy and the costume, and engage with your employees like you haven't been able to in a while. After all, the zombie in all of us needs to wake up.

Boo!

Power Thought
Don't GHOST Halloween this year!

Day 16:
Bloody Thursday

Currently, I am working with an organization to completely re-vamp two departments. They are the fastest growing business in the country in their industry, according to Inc. magazine, and they have grown from just fifteen employees to over eight-five in roughly two years. I had a talk with the CEO/owner of the business, and I asked him, "What was the turning point for your company's growth?"

"Bloody Thursday," he said, without missing a beat.

"That sounds ominous!" I replied.

He explained it like this: One day, he woke up and realized that about half his staff were the wrong fit for their roles. He gathered his top performers, and he rallied the troops. He said that he was letting go of the people that weren't pushing the company forward. Then, he developed the five company values: grit, live with grace, fear not, quality and excellence, and celebrate. From that point on, neither he nor his executive team make any decisions without consulting those values first.

From an outside perspective, when I walk into his office, there is lots of laughter. There is intense debate. There is compromise and a drive forward, and it is a pleasure and an honor to have this company as a client. Personally, I would call Bloody Thursday a success.

Power Thought
Sometimes the way forward depends
on getting your knuckles bloody.

Day 17:
Speaker School

As many of you know, I recently became a proud graduate of the Mikki Williams Speaker School. I flew to Naples, Florida and attended three days of speaker tutelage. In addition, I met some of the most amazing people in my class. I returned to work the following week with a new lease on life and my work, and with brand new connections to incredible new people.

Why am I discussing this?

Because professional development of your people is one of the most impactful ways to keep your employees happy and working for you. The website "Curious Desire" as a great article on fifteen benefits of professional development.[1]

All of my clients are worried about keeping their good employees, especially in the era of "The Great Resignation," and professional development is a fantastic way to ensure loyalty to you. In addition, you have employees with new and improved skills, like public speaking. With well-rounded, highly skilled employees on your team, you can accomplish any goal you choose. What could be better than that?

Power Thought

If you want to keep your people, teach them something new, like how to speak in public. That's a win-win!

---

1   https://curiousdesire.com/why-professional-development-is-important/

Day 18:
Where Are All the People?

For the past several months I have spoken to eleven groups of CEOs, and every group has asked the same questions: "Where are all the people?" "What secret island has all of the employees on it?" "The unemployment rate isn't zero, so where are all of the candidates?"

In February, The New York Times published an article that talks about part-time workers in this market, and many of those want full-time.[1]

Bottom line: There seems to be a disconnect between workers wanting full-time employment and the employers who want full-time workers. What is that disconnect?

Quite possibly, it's the new world of artificial intelligence, or AI. As a certified recruiter for Indeed.com, we have noticed that several of the job boards are sending resumes that are titled "Most Compatible"—even though most applications *are not*—which means that you aren't receiving the "less compatible" applications. In other words, some computer program in cyberspace is deciding *for* you whose application you get to see, and whose application you do not.

To be fair to Indeed.com and ZipRecruiter, most job boards have some sort of artificial intelligence to help employers sort resumes. They are trying to solve the problem that employers have been complaining about for years: being overwhelmed with applicants. In order to pare down the candidate pools, artificial intelligence has been incorporated by most job boards to pre-sort.

From a recruiting standpoint, I am giving my clients these five tips:

1) Don't just rely on job boards for recruiting

2) Utilize your website for applications

3) Utilize job fairs (there are a number of them going on!)

---

1   https://www.nytimes.com/2022/02/02/briefing/labor-shortage-part-time-workers-us.html

4) Use Craig's List, because it doesn't utilize artificial intelligence

5) Use physical job boards outside the office of your child's school or grocery stores

And finally, keep the faith. This will sort itself out. It always does.

Power Thought

Maybe the labor shortage is a computer glitch.

Day 19:
Why Your Employees Feel Unappreciated

In one of my recent Vistage meetings, a colleague brought up that she is hearing about a lot about employees who feel unappreciated, and she asked our group what we thought was going on.

Back when we had paper checks that we handed out to employees every Friday, or every other Friday, the boss would go around the office and hand each employee their check. The boss would look the employee in the eye, shake their hand and say, "Thank you for all the work you did this week! I so appreciate you!" Or something along those lines. Right then, the employee mentally connected the paycheck they received to their performance that pay period.

Now we have direct deposit.

The employee receives their pay in their account, which is convenient, but it eliminates that crucial appreciation conversation they could have had with their manager. There is a big disconnect between their paycheck and their performance.

One way to change this situation is to bring back the Friday "Thank You's." Every time your employees get paid, make it a habit to go to their desk—whether in office or virtual—and say, "Today is payday, and I wanted to tell you how much I appreciate you working for me. I couldn't do it without you."

Simple gratitude for them as employees should be associated with their paycheck. It isn't hard, and it matters to your people.

Power Thought

Use payday as an opportunity to connect with your people and express your gratitude.

Day 20:
When You Hired a Cultural Terrorist

"I hired a cultural terrorist," my client announced.

"A cultural terrorist?" I repeated.

"Yes," my client lamented. "She was our top salesperson and brought in a lot of money, but we simply couldn't keep her anymore. She made everyone's life here miserable, including mine. I lost a few key performers over her. So finally, I fired her."

"What happened next?" I asked, wide-eyed.

"You wouldn't believe it! First of all, the energy around here is lighter. People laugh more. There is more talking in the bullpen. The second layer of salespeople have also totally stepped up, and in the six weeks since I fired her, the next four salespeople have almost made up the difference. It's as if everyone knew what a trainwreck she was … and the awful stories that I am hearing about her … well, it was the right thing to do, and I should have done it months ago."

Like my client, when you hire an employee like this—or have one currently—the person will have a snowball effect. They only care about themselves. They use up resources. They are nasty to other employees. This is the M.O. of a cultural terrorist. That *one* employee can ruin your business, your reputation with your clients, and your ability to keep your people working for you. They aren't worth the money that they make for you, and it is time to let them go.

Power Thought

Don't sacrifice the entire staff for one cultural terrorist.
Cut bait and move on.

31

Day 21:
The Festering Fart After a Cultural
Terrorist

I followed up with the client who fired a cultural terrorist at his business, and I asked him how things were going.

He sighed, then said, "We have lots of issues. For example, now we have to complete all the projects that she sold. We are interacting with her clients and having to explain it without explaining it. Then we still have some of her supporters on staff, and the gossip is rampant. There is so much clean-up work. It is like a festering fart. The smell just lingers."

He is so right. If you have ever experienced firing a really bad employee, you know exactly how he feels. I suggested to him to get his team together and have a group conversation. After a situation like this, employees are asking two questions:

1) *What took you so long?* Employees generally identify a cultural terrorist long before management does, because the terrorist will kiss up to leadership, while crapping on those below and beside them.

2) *Is my job at risk too?* After someone is fired, it rattles every employee to the core, whether that person deserved to be fired or not.

Address these two questions like this: "It was time for us to part ways, and no one else is at risk of losing their job. I also need you all to help me get back on track for our year-end goals." Put a stop to the gossip and re-focus your team to the objectives. Then, do something fun as a group during work hours for team building. And, if the terrorist's supporters can't get onboard, they may also have to go.

Finally, hang tight, and have faith. The smell will dissipate eventually.

Power Thought

Your office will smell after firing a cultural terrorist,
but that festering fart will dissipate over time.

Day 22:
I Have *Another* Killer Tan!

Katy had three high school friends that I took on vacation every year. I absolutely loved going on vacation with them, and one year we went to Key West Florida to dig through the sand for seashells.

But every year, I worry about leaving on vacation. I worry that my clients will be mad that I am gone. I worry that something big is going to happen while I am not there. I worry that putting off the recruiting process will drag out longer than I want it to ... worry, worry and more worry.

Here is the truth: None of those worries ever come to fruition. As a matter of fact, the opposite is usually true. My clients are able to get more work done, because I am not there. They are relieved to have a break, and typically, the hiring process goes faster upon my return.

In addition, I am happier and more relaxed, and I have time to think about the hiring process from the 30,000-foot view, not just from the ground level.

Vacations have always been important! Whether you go somewhere exotic or have a "stay-cation" and spend the week at the pool working on your tan lines, you need a break. And I can say unequivocally that vacations are more important than ever. Not only are people burned out, but countless people are leaving their jobs. If you want to keep your best employees, my advice is always to let them go on vacation. And when they are gone, make sure that you are covering their work so that they can completely unplug.

We know that innovation comes from experiences outside the office. So, if you are worried that no work will get done, remind yourself that some of the best work happens when you and your team unplug.

When everyone returns, many will have killer tans, and you get solutions to big problems.

It's a win-win!

Power Thought

Vacations mean happier and more
productive employees.

Day 23:
When to *Not* Make Margaritas

When I owned my restaurant, we would have really busy times, and I would jump behind the counter and help my staff serve our customers. I was notorious for making margaritas by the bucket. I would go into the basement, get out the tequila, lime juice, triple sec, and apple juice (our secret ingredient), and literally create buckets of margaritas to serve with our amazing enchiladas and nachos.

While my staff was thrilled to have me help them serve our customers as quickly as possible, it was a short-term fix to a much larger issue. When we would get hit with a rush of people, as the owner of the company, my time was not best served by helping my staff in the moment. My time was best served by getting more staff on the floor, to help the customers get their orders. In other words, I needed to focus on the bigger picture; why we were short staffed at all in that moment?

Three years into owning the restaurant, I quit making margaritas. I refused to step back behind the bar to help, but instead I would begin calling more people on the floor. When I hired a general manager, it became his job to make those calls, and my job was to make sure that we had enough staff trained and ready to go for the busy times.

I see this all the time with my clients. They spend their time doing the extra work, when they should be spending time looking at the business as a whole. In other words, make your margaritas on Saturday, and focus on your whole business during the week.

¡Olé!

Power Thought
Observe the margarita makers.

Day 24:
Rethinking Hiring a Former Employee

I had a client call me last week with a question of whether or not to re-hire a former employee, and I am positive that he isn't the only one thinking about it. It also seems that employees are thinking about it too. According to Monster.com, 30 percent of former employees are trying to go back to their old jobs, with an additional 20 percent are thinking about it.[1]

I said to my client, "Well, it depends."

Here are some things to think about if you want to re-hire a former employee.

1. Did your re-hire "leave well" by giving you notice and wrapping up projects before their departure? Did they leave on good terms and help with creating a job description and/or training their replacement? Remember that the way your employee left you the first time will most likely be the way that they leave you the second time.

2. Will your re-hire add value to your current culture? Chances are your business has changed since your employee has left. Make sure that this person is still a fit for your business and the position.

3. Realize that it may be short term. If your re-hire left once, it is most likely because certain needs were not being met. Are those needs being met now? What has changed since their last period of employment with you? Make sure that you both address those un-met needs before bringing them back on board.

---

1   https://www.fastcompany.com/3057238/3-reasons-to-consider-returning-to-a-former-employer#:~:text=According%20to%20a%20recent%20Monster%20poll%2C%20nearly%2030%25,you%20simply%20send%20your%20resume%20into%20the%20void

One of my former colleagues in the restaurant industry often had kitchen staff that would periodically leave for more money, less hours, etc. He always thanked them for their service and let them pursue the new opportunity. Invariably, they would realize that life was not always greener on the other side of the fence and would try to come back. The ones that left well with integrity and honesty were hired back immediately. Those who left ungracefully, were not hired back.

Power Thought

Going back to an old employee is sometimes
just that: going backwards.

Day 25:
Can You Do a Cartwheel?

As many of you know, Katy has had several surgeries over the last twelve years and, as a kid, she never learned to do a cartwheel ... until last week.

Katy is now a Junior at the University of Miami and is right in the middle of finals. When she simply couldn't study one more minute, she and her friends went running through the park to get their Wheaties out. One of her friends executed a perfect cartwheel and encouraged Katy to try. She was nervous, but she tried. And succeeded! She was so excited!

Doing things that we have never done before is vital to our growth and longevity. It also boosts our confidence, which begets doing other things we have never done before. Then we have better creativity, better innovation, and more efficient progress. In the workplace, stepping into the unknown creates a bond with your employees that is unlike any other.

If you want to retain your people, to elevate culture, then encourage your employees to learn something new. Brush your teeth with your non-dominant hand, drive to work a different way, or attend a conference.

Soon enough, you and your whole team will be turning cartwheels!

Power Thought

Taking on new challenges is key to living a fulfilling life!

39

Day 26:
Wearing Jeans to the Gym

I interviewed one of my favorite clients for a high-level employee making in the six-figures. We then interviewed a gentleman who trashed his last boss, and then asked what type of product we sell. The name of the product is in my client's company name. He continued to ask questions that would have easily been answered if he had gone to the website for a mere five minutes. He chose not to do any research.

My client said, "He sounds like the type of guy that shows up to the gym in jeans."

Being prepared when you are interviewing for a job is simply a m-u-s-t! If you aren't willing to do even a little bit of research on the company with whom you are interviewing, that is a direct reflection of your (dis) interest in the company and working for them.

On the flip side, you as the employer must also be prepared for your interview. Know the interviewee's name. Have the job description in front of you, so that you can answer questions about expectations. Also, know ahead of time the pay, who the supervisor will be, what the training program will look like, and who will be in charge of that process.

Power Thought

Don't sweat hiring! Show up raring to go ...
in the right clothes, of course!

Day 27:
The Secret to Retention, Part 1:
Set the Stage

Imagine that you are starting your new job today. You have your new outfit, your briefcase, and of course a smile. You are so excited but also a bit nervous. You can't wait to get started; This is the dream job that you have wanted for a long time! You arrive five minutes early, open the door and walk up to the reception desk.

Scenario 1: There is no one to greet you. You sit for thirty minutes before someone comes out and says, "No one knew you were coming today!" You are placed in your office to fill out paperwork, and see no one else for hours. Then you are told that you will meet your hiring manager next week, because they are on vacation and oh by the way, your computer won't arrive for two weeks.

Or

Scenario 2: You arrive five minutes early and the receptionist says, "We are so excited that you are here!" Your new boss greets you enthusiastically, and shows you your office with a balloon tied to your chair and a welcome sign on your door. Your gleaming computer sits on your desk, and you are handed your itinerary for the week. After finding a place for your coat, briefcase and/or purse in your efficiently laid out office, your boss invites you into a conference room where they have a mini breakfast to introduce you to your team. Everyone rallies around you, and you feel touched, moved and inspired.

Which scenario will motivate you to stay longer at your job?

Here is the secret to retention: It starts from the first minute. If you want your employees to stay longer and be productive, you must set the stage for them to be successful from the very beginning. Most people naively believe that retention starts when an employee is ready to move on, with stay interviews, exit interviews and going away parties. But retaining employees is an ongoing effort from hiring the right person for the role, training them fully and completely, and incorporating them into their department as fast as possible.

Power Thought

Want your people to stay?
Value them before they even start.

*A big shout out to Cassy Nicholl for the topic!

Day 28:
The Secret to Retention, Part 2: Don't Keep Them Waiting

As most of you know, Katy is a nursing major at the University of Miami. Now that she is finishing her junior year, she started applying for internships, and in the second week of January, she was hired at a rehab center, which is a coveted place to work. Katy is fluent in Spanish, she has a 3.93 grade point average, and her clinical instructor told her that she would be a great nurse one day. As her mother, I think that she is a very qualified candidate ☺.

Katy's training for her new role took seven weeks to be scheduled. When she showed up on her first day at 8 a.m. as instructed, she waited in the lobby for an hour and a half for the hiring manager to show up. She finally decided to find the floor where she would be working and spent the rest of her shift taking vitals for patients on the floor. She spent almost the entire shift speaking Spanish to patients.

From a recruiting standpoint, I am completely appalled. She is the best of the brightest, and to be treated this way before she even started?

And companies wonder why they can't keep people ...

Power Thought
If you want to keep your employees,
start valuing them on day one.

Good morning, new employee!

We're so glad that you are here and we're excited to get going on your training. First, I would like to tell you about the hiring process that we went through to find you. Here are the numbers: we had 297 applicants; forty-nine people for the first interview; eleven second interviews; and three third interviews.

We chose you.

So, when you get frustrated—and you will—I want you to remember that we fought hard for you, and we want this to be a great experience for everyone. Make sure that you come to me with any questions along the way, and my team and I promise to do our best to provide a great work environment for you.

Ready to get started?

■   ■   ■   ■   ■

Can you imagine how you would feel if your new boss began your tenure this way? You would be overwhelmed by how much work was done to find you, and you would start off working with the feeling being valued, needed, and committed to.

Are you inspired? Think of how your new employee would feel!

Power Thought

According to Google, a new employee is 25 percent
more successful and they stay longer when they have
a meeting with their manager on their first day.[1]

---

1   https://www.process.st/onboarding-process/

Day 30:
The Secret to Retention #4: Puppies!

One Memorial Day weekend, Katy decided to foster a Mama dog and her four puppies. We spent twenty-four hours getting the house ready and drove to the Hylands area near Westminster, Colorado, to pick them up. Then, we spent Memorial Day doing nothing but sitting on the floor staring at the babies. We laughed loudly at the antics these puppies had for getting to the food source! Katy and I bonded over naming them: Mama Lily, Aspen and Barley, the boys, and Sage and Clover are the girls. We created lasting memories.

This experience reminded me of something vital in the workplace that many of us forget. Retention is so much easier when the employees are bonded and create lovely memories together. Most people generally don't want to leave their jobs because it is very stressful. Retention is simply providing the motivation to stay, and the best way to do that is this:

1) Provide a great place to work.

2) Provide great work.

3) Provide bonding experiences.

4) Pay well.

And I would now add volunteering together to save puppies!

Power Thought

It's a dog-eat-dog world out there.
Retaining your staff doesn't have to be ruff.

Accurate.

Steve Stifler
@StevStiffler

What being an adult feels like

♡ 83   10:55 PM - Dec 28, 2017

Day 31:
Want Great Employees? Hire a Lab.

Over the course of three years, our family rescued thirty-seven animals, fostered them, and got them adopted into great homes. One of my all-time favorites was a lab mix named Angel. And she was an angel! She was so sweet and loving, and she stayed right with you, no matter where you went.

We lived near a park, but in order to get there, we had to cross a very busy street. I always put a leash on Angel before walking over there, just to be safe. And frankly, it pissed her off. She would look up at me like, "Dude. I got this. Why the hell are you putting a leash on me?"

Recently, a good friend of mine quit her long-time job as a fundraiser for a high-powered non-profit. She ran the department that raised $8 million in 2021. She quit, because the executive director insisted that my friend show up at 8 am and stay until 5. After working there for 9 1/2 years, my friend was justifiably insulted. She gave a six months' notice to see if things would change. They didn't, so she left.

I have heard story after story of details, just like this one. When you, as the leader, put leashes on employees who have consistently proven themselves, they will start looking for another job. Then you lose a great employee, and you have to start over with someone new. What good does this do for anyone? My advice? Hire a "lab" that "walks" themselves, step back, and let them shine!

Power Thought

Leashes work during training. They do not work for
long-term, high-performing and trustworthy employees.

Day 32:
Cat Work

When a mangled, scruffy little kitten wandered into my daughter's apartment, she was hungry, tired, skinny and scared. Katy decided right then and there that she had to help this tiny being that she ultimately named, Dani Lou. Fast forward to today. Dani Lou is a fluffy, happy adventurous cat who fetches and sits for treats on command.

Over Christmas, Katy and Dani Lou came to visit me, and every morning Katy and I would compare notes on Dani Lou's night-time activities. Our conversations went like this:

Me: Did Dani sleep with you last night?

Katy: Yes, for a while. Then she left.

Me: What do you think she does all night?

Katy: Cat work.

Here is the bottom line: As the manager, you don't know what your staff does all day, every day. You especially don't know all the daily activities of your remote workers. And yet, they get their work done. They meet deadlines. Your clients are thrilled with the work that your company does, and they tell you so. Do you really need a detailed time report on what your staff is doing? Once your employees earn your trust, give them some free reign to learn something new.

You might be surprised at what they create.

Power Thought
Let them do their cat work.
Then, you can purr in satisfaction.

Day 33:
The Most Awkward Interview

Recently, the most awkward thing happened in an interview. I mean, it happens. And every time I think that I have seen it all, some candidate does or says something so completely random; and in this instance, unprofessional.

I was interviewing over the phone for a project manager. I called him on the phone and told him that my clients were listening in on his interview. He was very excited and said so.

Then, I heard him urinating. And flush. And wash his hands.

At least he washed his hands, but really?

There are so many things wrong with this scenario, it's hard to know where to begin. At the very least, this was a professional interview, and the candidate's behavior shows a gross lack of preparation. Do you want someone urinating while they are on the phone with your clients? I think not. Do I need to say it? Take care of your bodily functions before you call a client or have an interview!

For all of my clients: During an interview, you are seeing the best of the best of a candidate. So, ask yourself, *Is this really the best?*

For those of you who are seeking interview advice: Prior preparation prevents piss-poor performance. Literally.

Power Thought
You have *never* seen it all ... I promise.

Day 34:
Dani Lou and Mr. String

When Katy's cat, Dani Lou, literally walked in the door of Katy's apartment, she never left. She fetches toys and brings them back, and this cat sits for treats! Never seen anything like it.

One day, Katy heard the cat in the trash. Dani Lou pulled out a string that had come off a pair of sweatpants and began tossing it around the room and fetching it. She put it in her mouth and brought it to Katy to throw for her. When Dani catches her string and pulls it away, she prances back to Katy to have her throw it again. She has such pride in her steps! She has her head held high and dances her way back to you to show you what she has done. "Mr. String" goes everywhere with Dani Lou!

* * * * *

I had a bookkeeper one time who wanted to change the way that I did my books. I was hesitant at first, because I couldn't really understand what she wanted to do. What she described was way over my head, but she was so compelled to do it, I finally just let her. When she came back to me, she was *so* proud of the work that she had done. It was written all over her face when she pranced into my office to present my spotless books.

The key to happy employees is this: As often as possible, let your employees take the "string" and run with it. When you have employees on staff who take ownership of their work, and are allowed to pursue the best way to complete their tasks, they have immense pride in their work. They are happier, they stay longer, and they put their best foot forward, which means you can, too.

Power Thought

Don't string your employees along in a way that frustrates them. Instead, let each one take the string and lead you. You will both prance with pride.

Day 35:
What to Do When Tragedy Strikes

Recently, Colorado lost almost 1000 homes in an awful fire. A client, who had employees that lost their homes, frantically called me and said, "I don't know what to do! How do I help my people?"

So, I put together some suggestions.

1) Pick up the phone and call each person. They need to hear from you. They need to know that you are going to support them and that you have their back. They may not be in a place to call you back immediately, so don't read into it if they don't. Call once every week or two, with no expectation of a call back.

2) Take action. Don't ask them what they need, just provide it. For example, when Katy was in the hospital the first time, my friend, Beth, sent a ton of food to our hospital room. She didn't ask; she just did it. Also, a friend sent a handmade blanket to the hospital. I have it on my lap as I am typing this, and I have never forgotten these beautiful acts of kindness. Your employees won't either.

3) Find items to give. When someone has lost their home, "stuff" isn't what they need, because they have no place to put it. Take them food and water; bottled water, fruit, nuts, crackers, peanut butter, bread, etc. The people who came to the donation center where I donated my time asked for blankets, towels, socks, underwear and warm clothes.

4) Donate money to the family directly. In the Boulder 2012 fire, $650,000 went to the Red Cross, but the families didn't see that money. If you have a friend or employee who was directly affected, donate to them or take the initiative to set up a GOFUNDME account.

5) Listen. Just listen. Your friend, family member or employee needs a safe outlet to process their heavy emotions when a tragedy strikes. You don't have to fix their situation for them; in fact, you can't. But you can be a sounding board and provide support when they need it most.

6) Finally, take care of yourself, so that you can be available for them. Rally the troops and check in regularly. We all need each other, and your employee will never forget the action that you took on their behalf.

Power Thought

Put on your oxygen mask first, and then help
your employee out with the suggestions above.
Your act of kindness will always be remembered.

Day 36:
Need Staff? Raise Your Standards.

"I have a problem," confessed one of my favorite clients on a conference call.

"Oh yeah? What is it?" I asked.

"I have too many employees," she said with a sigh.

Well, *that's* one I haven't heard before!

■   ■   ■   ■   ■

Meet Lindsay Shaw, from Lindsay's Boulder Deli and Haagen Daas. She and I did some hiring and management consulting in 2018, and she has since gone on to hire and train successfully on her own. I called her randomly to find out how she was doing, especially during a labor shortage for restaurant staff. She has the opposite problem of most other restaurants; she has former employees coming back to her and begging for hours.

Which presents the question: Why is that?

Lindsay: "I think that when you are short on staff, it is tempting to lower your standards. But when you do that, the good people will leave to find a better place to work. The 'great' employees want to work in a place with high standards; a culture that values being the best and the brightest, and because they are so great, they can get hired wherever they go."

While it seems counterintuitive, when there is a shortage of staff, do *not* lower your standards. Hold those great employees in high esteem and hold out for the best candidates. Then you can be like Lindsay with amazing staff, low drama, happy customers and a healthy and thriving work environment.

Happy hiring!

Power Thought

Great staff thrive with high standards.
Bad staff thrive with low standards.

Day 37:
Where Are All the People?
Here's the Good News...

Over the past several months, every news outlet has published articles about labor shortages, no one to hire, and the Great Resignation. These articles are full of gloom and doom, and of course, there is panic on all levels about how to hire and how to retain employees. Instead of buying into that fear, I would like to pass on to you three pieces of really good news.

#1: When there are lots of people leaving companies, that means there are lots of people to hire. If you are getting applications, then you don't have a recruiting problem. You have a selection problem.

SOLUTION: Focus on your interview process and your application process. Are you making it too hard to apply? Are you following up with people quickly? Is your ad inspiring, or is it yawn-worthy?

#2: Over the last year of new hires, 58 percent took a pay cut to go to their new position.[1]

So, more money isn't the answer to get people to stay.

SOLUTION: work on your culture. If you have crappy managers and a fear-based leadership style, you aren't going to be successful in hiring.

#3: Of the folks who changed jobs, 78 percent are happier that they did. What this means to hiring managers is that if your interview process is solid and your culture is supportive, then your new hires will be happier and more productive at work.

---

[1] https://www.bizjournals.com/bizwomen/news/latest-news/2021/10/covid-19-career-change-pandemic-happier.html?utm_source=st&utm_medium=en&utm_campaign=nch&ana=e_n_bizwomen_tease

Bottom line: The workforce is changing, and business owners have to change with it. If you enhance your culture and get rid of toxic people, you will hire better and retain more employees without spending more money.

Power Thought

Best. News. EVER!

Day 38:
Do You Have Any Reservations
About Hiring Me?

After I conducted an interview, I asked the candidate if they had any questions, then I waited for the dreaded question: "Do you have any reservations about hiring me?"

I hate this question.

I know why candidates ask it. Every article about interviewing tells candidates to, "Ask for feedback" in the interview, so that the candidate can "address any issues."

Why do I hate it so much? Because it puts the employer on the spot. The fact is we can't give feedback to the candidate, because if given poorly, it opens the door for potential lawsuits and complaints. There is zero benefit to the company for giving feedback to a candidate, and the company must consider the employees already on payroll. Also, the candidate typically isn't truly open to feedback at this point because they are under so much stress. From my perspective, pointing out someone's flaws while in an interview is just cruel. How do you say to someone, "I can't hire you because you come across as a complainer"? What the candidate will say is, "I'll change!" because they want or need the job.

Bottom line: No one wins in that situation. It is incredibly uncomfortable for all parties involved.

The way I avoid this question during an interview is by naming the elephant in the room: "We have to talk about you behind your back before I can answer that question." And usually, everyone laughs, and we move on.

I don't know who decided this question was a must for candidates, but it does *nothing* to promote a good working relationship with your potential employer. If you are a candidate looking for a job, don't ask this question. And if you are an employer who is asked this in an interview, name the elephant and move on.

Being uncomfortable is not a good thing in an interview, so don't promote it.

Power Thought

Do you have any reservations about hiring me?
None that I can discuss with you.

Day 39:
HOAs & Hiring

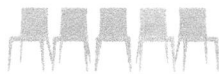

I have to chuckle when I think about a few of my neighbors approaching me to sit on the HOA Board as the Secretary/Treasurer. Actually, to be more accurate, it was an ambush; I was supposed to have a beer with the President, and she also brought the VP for a "meeting" to "invite" me to join the Board.

She then proceeded to tell me all of the problems of being on the Board, namely that once you are on the Board it is hard to roll off. The neighbors complain, the irrigation system needs to be replaced, and the hail damage to the roofs was extensive. In addition, folks are on a fixed income, so raising rates isn't really an option.

After all of this, I asked her, "So, why do you do it?"

Her answer surprised me. "Because I love it."

If you have read *any* of my blogs, or ever heard me speak, you know that I preach loudly the mistake of over-selling the position for which you are hiring. But there is also the problem of turning people off by talking too much about all the issues. I left that conversation asking myself, *Why on earth would I do this job?* And the answer is, "Because I love it."

■　■　■　■　■

When you are writing your ad for people to come on board, you must have the right mix of inspiration and practicality. You must address the issues, but not in a way that scares people off. You need to talk about the perks of the job, but not in a way that makes you seem desperate.

As for me and the HOA? I'm still thinking about it. Stay tuned!

Power Thought
Your job ad must have the right mix of
inspiration and practicality. Every time.

Day 40:
Want to Hire Better? Foster Dogs.

Several years ago, our family fostered a Boxer dog named Helen. She was blind in one eye and was considered aggressive. Therefore, she couldn't be around other animals or children. Then, she blew out her knee and had to have it replaced. As we were rehabilitating that knee, the other knee blew out and it had to be replaced.

As a foster family, it was our job to come up with an Ideal List for Helen's *furever* home. I really struggled with this one. How were we ever going to find someone who was going to adopt a dog that had two replaced knees, who was blind in one eye, didn't get along with other animals, and shouldn't be around children? It seemed so daunting to even think about it.

Sound familiar?

Every client that I work with tells me that their position is going to be really hard, because they are looking for someone "really unique." Their job is going to be so hard to fill, because they are looking for a unicorn. But really, the hardest part of a search is being patient. You have to wait for the right fit to come along, and in the world of, "I must have it right now!" patience is in short supply.

Lo and behold, we found the perfect home for our beloved Helen, and she lived out her days with a family that thought she hung the moon.

You, too, can find your amazing new hire. It isn't as "ruff" as you think.

Power Thought
It is a dog-eat-dog world out there.
But with patience, you can find your amazing hire!

Day 41:
Paddleboarding in Florida

Recently, I spent two glorious weeks in Florida on the ocean. One day, Katy decided that she wanted to go paddleboarding. I couldn't have been more unenthusiastic.

"Come on, Mom! It'll be fun!" she said, while running towards the enormous boards. She hauled one out to the ocean and promptly hopped on.

I hesitantly scooted the board in the water. I cautiously looked in the water underneath the board, convinced that Jaws would leap out and bite me. I awkwardly climbed on the board and immediately fell right off. I *so* didn't want to do this! But by this time Katy was halfway around the bend, and I didn't want to be left out.

So, I tried again and again. Finally, I got some traction and paddled out to where Katy was. I still hadn't stood up on the board but sitting and paddling was pretty okay. Katy yelled, "See Mom... it's fun!"

Pfft. "I mean, it's alright," I grumbled.

Then, I got over myself. I stood up. I teeter-tottered trying to find my balance, until a wave from a boat knocked me down. I got back up, planted my feet, found my center, and was able to paddle around. The sun was warm, the wind was light, the ocean was so blue, and I was with one of the best people in my life. Total perspective shift.

■   ■   ■   ■   ■

Learning something new is hard. You feel awkward and hesitant. You fall down. You look funny. But then, you get back up and you try again. This is how innovation occurs! This is how new ideas are created, and this is how you stay mentally sharp.

So, get on that board. Plant your feet. Find your center and enjoy the world. You won't regret it.

Power Thought

Learning something new is no walk in the park.
Do it anyway.

Day 42:
Buying Blue Jeans & Hiring

Do you realize how many types of blue jeans there are in this world?

Straight leg, vintage style, loose fit, skinny jeans, mom jeans, ultra-high rise, high rise, mid-rise, low rise, ultra-low rise, boyfriend jeans, boot cut, cropped, ankle, extra-long, extra short, curvy, petite, tall. And I haven't even started on colors: white wash, dark wash, light blue, dark blue, navy ... the list is endless!

You can literally have any type of jean that you want. The question is: What kind do you want?

■ ■ ■ ■ ■

I have an amazing client who sent me an email comparing employees to blue jeans, and I thought this was a great analogy.

The purpose of a pair of jeans is to cover your tush ... that's it. But most people I know have a pair of jeans that is their all-time favorite. They have been washed multiple times, so they are soft, they are the right length, not too tight, not too loose, and you feel like a million dollars in them!

Can you wear another pair of jeans? Sure, but they aren't the same, are they?

■ ■ ■ ■ ■

My client asked this question: "Can't I hire a pair of blue jeans, even though they aren't my favorite?"

Of course you can! You can hire a substandard pair of blue jeans, and there are times that you need to do that. For example, you have so much business that you hire a "sub-standard pair of jeans" to just get you through the tough times. You know that those "jeans" won't stay around forever, but they are good for now. You can also hire a "pair of jeans" that don't fit quite right, but you need them for a weekend trip.

Just know that those "jeans" are short-term; don't expect them to stay around forever.

But at the end of the day, your favorite "pair of jeans" set the standard for all other "jeans."

My thought? If they aren't a perfect fit, put them back on the shelf and keep looking.

Power Thought

There is nothing better than your favorite
pair of jeans or your favorite employee.
Hold out for more just like that.

Day 43:
The War Over Remote Work

Since the dawn of computers and the internet, workers have been wanting to work from home at least part of the time. However, employers wanted all employees in the office. Some employers would allow working from home on an occasional basis for total rockstar employees, or those who were part of the C-suite, but mostly, employees were required to come to the office.

Enter COVID. And suddenly nearly everyone was forced to work from home.

Now, we are in this tug-of-war where employees who worked from home mostly liked their schedule or at least want a more flexible option, like a hybrid work schedule.

Most employers are adamantly opposed to this. Why? Because employers don't trust their employees. Or, from my perspective, they don't trust their hiring process.

If you have a fantastic employee that you don't have to manage, life is great. You know the ones: they communicate well, they meet deadlines, they solve problems, your customers *love* them. Then, you don't care if they work from home! They can do whatever they want, because you know at the end of the day, the work is getting done and clients are pleased.

But, if you hire a crappy employee who works from home, it is damn near impossible to micro-manage them if they aren't in the office. Therein lies the rub.

In order to offer work-from-home options and feel good about it, an employer must have a solid hiring process in place. The right employee is going to be effective, no matter where they work, and the wrong employee will get nothing done, no matter where they work. It really is that simple and straight forward.

Power Thought

Solve the work-from-home dilemma by improving your hiring process. Then you can work from home, too!

Day 44:
Don't Fan Boy!

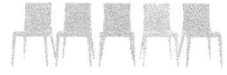

When my interview team conducted a second interview with a gentleman, he totally knocked the ball out of the park. He was prepared, asked great questions and he had the demeanor and skill set that we were looking for.

My client wanted to hire him right then and there. I said no, because we had a third interview to go through to completely finish the interview process. He wasn't very happy with me, but he conceded.

We set up the third interview with this candidate, who showed up late. His demeanor was condescending, and it was very clear this wasn't the job that he ultimately wanted.

My client was stunned.

Later, over tacos, my client said, "I think I got it now. You can't Fan Boy over a candidate."

Nailed it.

The third interview is such a make-it-or-break-it event. Why? Because the candidate has relaxed. They realize that they are close to getting a job offer, so they let down and show you their true selves, warts and all. It can be truly mind-boggling to watch, especially when the candidate turns out to be the wrong fit. As one of my clients so eloquently stated, "Thank *God* for the third interview!"

The lesson, as it often is in business, is to finish the process and don't Fan Boy. You can't be obsessed with a candidate; you have to be obsessed with the process. Ultimately, this leads to hiring the right fit.

Power Thought

Fan Boy the process, not the candidate.
You can Fan Boy over the candidate after
they become a rockstar employee.

*** A Big shoutout to Chris Ekurt for this idea!

Day 45:
Bad Hires, Prince Charming, and Frogs

I had a potential new client call me wanting to discuss my services, and he asked if I conducted confidential searches. He further explained that he needed to fire the person in a top-level role in his company, but he had to have a body in that seat. "Can you help me?" he asked.

My answer? No, I do not do confidential searches, and here is why: You can't find Prince Charming while you are married to the frog.

When you begin a new search under the cloud of secrecy, lies and lack of transparency, that is the type of person you will attract. Keeping a secret is really hard, especially when you are interacting with the person that you *know* you are going to fire. You will most likely slip up. Or the candidate, who instinctively knows that their head is on the chopping block, is likely looking for a new job. What happens when they see your ad? And with all of the focus on getting fired/finding someone new, you can be sure that this person isn't doing their job well anyway.

In addition to the secrecy, think about the tone this sets for all of your other employees. How will they feel when they find out that you treated someone on their team in such a shady way? Do you think they will stay with you? Think again.

Letting someone go from your team is horrible for all parties. But putting it off for any length of time only creates additional bad will, drama and disruption.

Bottom line? Cut ties with the frog as soon as possible. Re-group, bolster your existing team, and hold out for the *right* person. There is nothing more satisfying than working with people who all want to be there.

Power Thought

Break up with the frog to make room
for the prince/princess.

Day 46:
Promote A Killer Tan!

While interviewing people for my clients, I am asking candidates about their vacation plans. I am super pleased to find out that people are taking time off this year! Thank the stars!

As the world is opening up, and people are leaving their houses for the first time in over a year, there is this feeling of restlessness and, "I have to get out of here for a while!"

Vacations have always been important, whether you go somewhere exotic or have a "stay-cation" and spend the week at the pool working on your tan lines. However, taking a vacation is more important than *ever*.

Not only are people burned out, a huge number are leaving their jobs. If you want to keep your best employees, my advice is always to let them go on vacation. And when they are gone, make sure their work is covered so that they can completely unplug.

We know that innovation comes from experiences outside the office. So, if you are worried that no work will get done, remember that some of the best work happens when you and your team unplug.

They get a killer tan, and you get solutions to big problems.

Win/win.

Power Thought

Taking a vacation increases happiness and productivity!
And your tan!

Day 47:
It Takes All Kinds

No two people are alike, and we all have strengths and weaknesses. This is important because it takes all kinds of people to make the world go round. What you are good at doing is very different from what I am good at doing, and this is how innovation occurs. Our diversity is how we solve problems.

Here are three hilarious examples of our differences:

1. I interviewed a candidate for a Senior Financial Analyst position for one of my clients:

   Me: "How comfortable are you using Excel?"

   Candidate: She responded with a short laugh, "Well, if this tells you anything, I have an Excel spreadsheet on how to care for my plants."

2. Conversation with a client:

   Client: "How is your day going today?"

   Me: "It's great! I am interviewing seventeen people today! I am *so* in my happy place!"

   Client: "That is because you are *sick*!"

3. Conversation with Katy:

   Me: "How is school going?"

   Katy: "Great! We are studying the plague, and it is riveting!"

   In all three of these examples, someone has a strength that makes the other person want to throw up. Isn't that just lovely?

Power Thought

When hiring, make sure that you hire people with strengths that are different than yours. That is how to become more efficient and productive. After all, it takes all kinds of people to make the world go round, and, perhaps more importantly, move your company to the places you want it to go.

Day 48:
Everyone Needs a Katy

I hate to shop. I do mean that I *hate* to shop! I hate everything about it: the time, the energy, having to try it on, having to take it back if it doesn't fit. There is *nothing* that I like about shopping.

I recently traveled to see one of my favorite clients out of state. She greeted me enthusiastically and said, "You look so cute! Where do you get your clothes?"

Funny story.

Last fall Katy called me from a store and said, "I found a really cute sweater that I think you might like. I am going to buy it and bring it home for you to try on. If you don't like it, I will bring it back and return it." I did like it! A lot! So, I kept it. Then, Katy went back to that store and bought me some more clothes. I tried them on and kept most of them. I had a new wardrobe, and I never had to shop.

Bliss!

My client turned to me after I told her this story and said, "Everybody needs a Katy."

She is so right.

Katy has already gone shopping for me for summer clothes, because she was worried that I wouldn't have anything to wear.

Katy saw a project that needed to be done. She told me what she was going to do to solve the problem, and then she went out and did just that—solved the problem. We joke now that she is my personal shopper, and several of my friends have jokingly stated that they need her to shop for them, too.

Can you imagine having an employee that sees a problem, then tells you how they are going to solve it for you?

When my client told me, "Everybody needs a Katy!" she wasn't joking.

And I do look really cute in my new clothes.

A win-win!

Power Thought

A really great employee takes a project and runs with it.
"Shop" for candidates like that.

Day 49:
The Mermaid House

When I started looking for a new home, the timing couldn't have been worse. The real estate market in Colorado was stupid, and I am not usually known for my patience.

During my search, I encountered this house that had pink walls and a 3-D mermaid sticking out of the wall (**see photo**). The place was dirty, not staged well, had a half-eaten box of pop tarts in the basement closet, and a life-sized portrait of Mother Teresa with a kneeling rug where the dining room table should be. The office had blood red walls, and the floor-to-ceiling fireplace had been totally blocked by over-grown vines.

I turned to my realtor and said emphatically, "Oh *hell* no."

My realtor, Heather Slump, disagreed with me. She said, "It's just paint and carpet, Beth. Easily fixable. Plus, the layout is perfect for you, and this place is very well-built." She was right. She started talking to me about possibilities, and she created a picture of what this place could be, minus the mermaid. I got really excited!

I moved in shortly thereafter. I bought the place under asking price, and I was the only offer. This is the single best place I have ever lived!

■ ■ ■ ■ ■

You can have the same experience with employees. You are never going to find great people, if all you do is focus on the resume. If all you ever do is look at experience, degrees and university names, you can miss the magical "merfolk" that come across your desk. Make waves with your hiring process! Look outside the box!

Imagine the possibilities; you will be so glad you did.

And for the Mermaid house? Things are going along swimmingly.

Power Thought

You can have any employee that you want by focusing
on the magic of your hiring process. Your mermaid/
merman is right around the jetty.

Day 50:
Extending Grace to Employees During a Pandemic

Last week, I Interviewed a woman for a senior level position during COVID, and immediately her child began to scream. Obviously flustered, the woman apologized profusely and said something to me that I will never forget: "You know, I don't know how people do this. I can't even ask my neighbor to come watch my child for fifteen minutes while I have an interview. As matter of fact, I can't even ask my own mother to come over to spend time with her grandchild!"

I then asked her how she managed her childcare versus working at her current position, and she said, "Luckily, I have a very flexible boss who lets me work the hours that I need to in order to get the job done. I work from 8 p.m. to 2 a.m. and then when my child takes a nap."

Wow.

Even as a parent, I don't think the full impact of how hard it is to have small children and a job with absolutely *zero* childcare help until I spoke to this candidate. According to Family Friendly NC, 4.3 million parents may have to leave the workforce due to the COVID pandemic.[1] If you have great employees who are parents, I strongly encourage you to reach out to them often. Ask them how things are going, then ask them how *you* can help. We know that employees who feel seen, heard and valued, stay at jobs longer, and my hunch is these people need to feel this now more than ever.

In any business, turnover hurts the bottom line. If your employee is a good one, reaching out is the best way to keep them afloat. You need them, they need you, and it is also the right thing to do as a human being.

---

1 https://familyforwardnc.com/saving-hospitality-employees-a-family-friendly-way/#:~:text=As%20parents%20try%20to%20balance%20working%20from%20home%2C,their%20jobs%20to%20take%20care%20of%20their%20families

Power Thought

You'll increase your bottom line by staying in contact
on a personal level with your employees.

Day 51:
When You Hire, Your Default Should Be, "No"

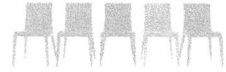

I was interviewing with one of my favorite clients, and we were talking about general hiring practices. I said, "When you talk to a client, you want to always say, "Yes." You want to solve their problems, because that is how you get to do the work that you love. That is also is how you make money, which gives you the opportunity to grow. "

My brilliant client replied, "Exactly. When talking to clients, your default should be yes. But when you are hiring your default should be no."

He is totally right.

Hiring is about rejection. Think about it. You receive 300 resumes for a job, and you will reject at least 299 of them, if not all 300. Then, you receive another 300, and the process starts again.

The reason that hiring is so hard for business leaders is because their default is set to yes. When a client comes to you for help, you want to say yes. It's fun!

As hard as that can be for some people, the reality is, you just can't do that in hiring.

Power Thought

When hiring, make a conscious effort
to switch your default from yes to no.

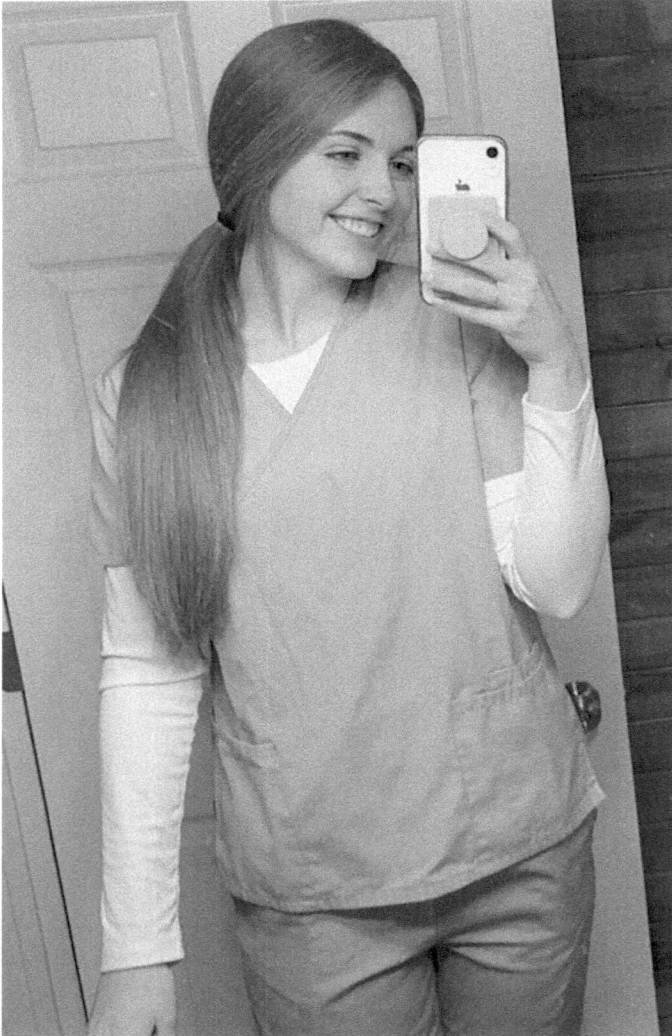

Day 52:
The Non-Interview

When Katy applied for a job as a Personal Care Aide, she knew she would be going to a client's home who has some sort of disability. As a future nurse, Katy wanted to get some practical, real-world experience before she started her clinicals. Really smart on her part.

She applied online to a company with her resume and targeted cover letter. The woman emailed Katy within hours and asked her for a phone interview the following day. Here is how the conversation went:

Interviewer: Do you have a reliable car?

Katy: Yes.

Interviewer: Do you want part-time?

Katy: Yes.

Interviewer: Does this hourly rate work for you?

Katy: Yes.

Interviewer: Then you have the job! I will send you some paperwork to fill out, and we will call you for orientation after your background check comes back. Do you have any questions?

After the interview, Katy called me and said, "You are probably appalled."

"Uh, yes. Yes, I am. What kind of an interview is that? And for taking care of someone with a disability in their home? I am horrified."

When you hire out of desperation, you make mistakes two-thirds of the time. This company got lucky with Katy. She is smart, kind and responsible. She will make a *great* aide to her clients. And because the company gets lucky, they won't dig deep to figure out a way to really interview people effectively. And thus, the cycle continues.

If you are looking for front line, hourly workers, I have a shorter interview process that is highly effective, and it can turn the tide from desperate to visionary in a very short period of time. Think about it and reach out if you want to discuss. Your future company will thank you for it.

Power Thought

A "non-interview" is the road to "non-success" in hiring.

Day 53:
How Do You Stop Waiters from
Applying to Your C-Suite Position?

I graduated from college before the internet. (I am totally dating myself here!) I put on my panty hose (barf), printed my short resume on good quality paper, and drove to company #1 to see if I could talk to someone about getting a job. Then, I drove to company #2 and did the same thing. If I went to five or six companies per day, it was a good day! In other words, I had to be strategic about applying for jobs.

In this day and age, you can apply for a hundred jobs on a Sunday morning in your favorite pj's and fuzzy bunny slippers. There is no strategy required on the candidate's part.

Recently, one of my favorite people on the planet called to me to ask me, "How do I stop waiters from applying to my high-level job?"

The short answer is, "You can't."

Power Thought
Quit worrying about what you *can't* control
and start working on what you *can* control.

Day 54:
Become a Member of the Casserole Community

When I grew up, if we knew of anyone who was going through a major life event, we took a casserole over to their house. We took casseroles to people who were sick, who had a relative that died, had a surgical procedure or when someone had a baby. It was our way of showing support for people in our community. It was how we showed people that we cared about them, and that they could count on us when it mattered. We were a part of their "Casserole Community."

When I contracted COVID-19 over the Christmas holidays, 2020, it was a brutal three weeks. At 10:30 p.m. on Christmas Eve, I was having trouble breathing and decided to call 9-1-1. I sat down on the bed to rest for a minute until I could gather enough strength to go get my cell phone, and the next thing I knew, it was 5:30 in the morning. All the lights were on, and I had made it through the night. I had turned a corner.

At one point, I was feeling particularly sorry for myself for being sick over the Christmas break, and my girlfriend texted me to see if I was okay. I texted back that I was getting better, and I appreciated her checking in. She offered to send me groceries on Instacart. She was not the only one. My friends and neighbors showed up (virtually) in droves to send food, to check in, to offer moral support. My self-pity turned into gratitude for my "Casserole/Instacart Community."

Here is the deal: Whether we are in the middle of a global pandemic, a major life event, a personal or work-related issue, or we are simply feeling down, we *need* each other. So, ask yourself this question: Who is in your Casserole Community? Whose Casserole Community are you a part of? Who can you count on when you need help/support? Who can count on you? Even in the best of times, we all need a community, and even more so when things are not going well. However, being there for each other can make the situation infinitely more bearable.

Power Thought

Think about who needs you to order them
some groceries online. Or think about two people
that you need to check in on today. I'll guarantee
you will make someone's day with a small gesture
of kindness and caring.

Day 55:
Feeling Desperate When Hiring?
Here's Why ...

I love Grape Nuts. I mean, I *love* them! I have been eating them for over half my life. They are so versatile! I eat them with fruit, with yogurt, with fruit and yogurt, with a little milk at night before bed. Swipe some almond butter on a banana and dip it into a bowl of Grape Nuts and eat it. Yum!

One evening, during COVID I noticed that I was getting low. When I went to Safeway to buy more, they didn't have any. They didn't have any the next week either. Sprouts didn't have any, nor do they carry Grape Nuts. When I asked the woman at the counter, she said haughtily, "That is a *Post* product. We don't carry any of Post products."

Okay then.

By the next month, I was getting really desperate, so I visited my trusted friend, Amazon. They had two boxes for $20.00 and an extra $10.00 for shipping. I am not doing that! The next week, no Grape Nuts at Safeway, and the online price was now $60.00! Are you kidding me? And I was not the only one to notice.[1]

The problem was that at this point, I was actually considering it! I told myself that I would skip Happy Hour that week and buy the damn Grape Nuts.

Ugh!

On Monday, I sashayed into Safeway, and there on the shelf like a beacon of light were two boxes of Grape Nuts. The angels wept and the choir sang. I bought both of those bad boys for a whopping $4.99 a box, saved myself $50.00 and I didn't have to skip Happy Hour.

Score!

■   ■   ■   ■   ■

---

1   https://www.usatoday.com/story/money/food/2021/01/27/grape-nuts-shortage-breakfast-cereal-supply-coronavirus-demand/4259281001/

When you are searching for your right candidate, you might feel like I did about my Grape Nuts. You look and look. You "post" your job ad on Indeed.com, on LinkedIn, on Monster ... anywhere that you think might have your person. You are desperate. You start to get a tightness in your chest. Did they quit making my beloved Grape Nuts or is there a war on talent?

Then, when you least expect it, your prayers are answered—a gift from the Hiring Gods—or in my case, the cereal makers.

Power Thought

I want you to be a "cereal" interviewer, not a "cereal" hirer. Hold out! Be patient. Your dream hire is coming!

Day 56:
Never Use THIS Word!

I flew to Austin to interview a candidate for a third interview in a blinding snowstorm. While things went very smoothly in Denver, they did *not* go smoothly in Austin. Once we arrived at the airport, we circled for about an hour, until our pilot announced that we were being diverted to San Antonio; the airport in Austin closed to deal with the snow. To be fair, Austin got a few inches of snow that they hadn't seen in 25 years.

We arrived in San Antonio, the pilot said that we were going to get re-fuel, then fly back to Austin. "It will be a quick fifteen-minute flight" he said. We circled the airport for forty-five minutes, when he announced that we would be diverted to Houston. *No one* on the plane wanted to go to Houston! Then, the pilot said, "We need 1 ¼ mile of visibility. We have 1 mile. So, we are going to try and land the plane."

Excuse me?

A college-aged girl named Emily was sitting next to me, and with wide eyes she looked at me and said, "*Try*? Did he say, 'T-r-y'?"

He did. Emily and I held hands as the pilot *tried* to land the plane. Obviously, he did. And actually, it was one of the smoother landings I have experienced.

According to Inc. Magazine, people who use the word "try" have given themselves permission to fail, and this causes the rest of us to find them uncredible.[1] What if I said to you, "I will *try* to hire a great employee for you." Those words don't inspire confidence, do they?

Work on eliminating "try" from your vocabulary. And for those smart alecks in my network, don't respond to me with, "I'll try"!

Power Thought

"Do or do not. There is no try." – Yoda

---

1   https://www.inc.com/geoffrey-james/3-words-that-guarantee-failure.html

Day 57:
When Did You Last Buy Pants?

I have been conducting video interviews for almost a decade. Early on in my video career, I did what a lot of people do, and I wore a blazer and my pajama pants. Except in the middle of the interview, I realized that my file with my resumes was on top of the filing cabinet next to my desk. I stood up to grab the file, and the candidate said, "Nice pajama bottoms!"

My pj pants had crushed beer cans on them.

Needless to say, I have never done that again!

These days, I am not the only one who has hidden their favorite jammies underneath the desk. According to CNN Business, pants sales have plummeted since the beginning of the pandemic, but pajama sales have skyrocketed by 143 percent![1] And according to bizjournals.com slippers are having their moment too.[2]

Take it from me: While those pj bottoms might be really comfortable, it is really easy to get *too* comfortable. If you want to present yourself in a highly professional way, you must put on real clothes. The phrase "dress for success" is a mantra for a reason.

So, make sure that you buy—and wear!—real pants when you are on a video call.

You can, however, wear your fuzzy bunny slippers on your feet. I may or may not be wearing mine.

Power Thought
Clothes set the tone for how you want other
people to perceive you.

---

1 https://www.cnn.com/2020/05/12/business/coronavirus-online-shopping/index.html
2 https://www.bizjournals.com/bizwomen/news/latest-news/2021/01/slippers-having-a-moment-during-work-from-home-win.html?utm_source=st&utm_medium=en&utm_campaign=nch&ana=e_n_bizwomen_tease

Day 58:
Terrible at Hiring? Good.

I had a conversation with one of my clients who was telling me that he is terrible at hiring. I said "Good."

He looked at me like I had grown a third head, and said, "Why would you say that?!?"

"Because if you have trouble with hiring, it is usually because you are a good human being and you want to give people chances."

Here is the bottom line: We are biologically wired to connect to people. That is how our species has lasted all this time. We are connected in groups, and we help each other out. Hiring, though, is about rejection. You get 300 resumes. You will reject at least 299 of them, if not all 300. Then, you get 300 more resumes, and the process starts all over again. We *hate* to reject people! It isn't in our DNA to do so. We hire someone not good for the role, and we hang onto them forever because we hate to reject people.

I want you to hire the right fit and be a good human being to *that* person. I want you to be surrounded by great employees, so that you can be good to everyone on your staff. You can coach, mentor, and teach to people who love their jobs and are happy to be working for you.

If you are terrible at hiring, then you are a great human being.

I really like that about you!

Power Thought
It's better to be a great human being
than a good hiring manager.

Day 59:
Are Dating & Hiring the Same?

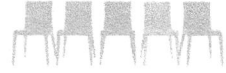

Two weeks ago, I had the following conversation with Katy.

Katy: "I am posting your online dating profile tonight."

Me (horrified): "*Why?*"

Katy: "Because you aren't getting any younger."

Sigh.

After about a week, I had over 100 invitations to meet. Don't get too excited: The one that chased me the most was named Scooter, and he was missing several teeth.

Those of you who haven't been in the dating pool for a while are probably wondering, how does this experience relate to hiring? In a surprising number of ways, it is exactly the same. You create an Ideal List for your next candidate/date with attributes, like honesty, integrity and bi-cuspids. You put together a job/relationship description. You write your ad/profile. You wade though resumes/profiles. And then you start interviewing/dating.

The key difference between dating and hiring is that in hiring someone for a job, you as the employer, have all the power. You dictate the criteria, the Ideal List, the interview process, the salary, the title, the office/remote arrangement, and the job. Your potential employee has very little say in any of this until they get hired.

In dating, the two people come together as equals, each with the ability to adjust to the needs of the other. And this is a very big difference between dating and hiring.

And as far as Scooter with his missing incisors? Alas, we will not be meeting. I wish him the very best of luck in his search.

Stay tuned!

Power Thought
Make sure your interview process has teeth!

Day 60:
Zoom Zombies in the Workplace

To say that life is strange is an understatement. The virtual workplace is a struggle! Do you log into Zoom and see Zombies disguised as employees? Those lifeless bodies that stare off into space? Does it feel like your company culture is dead?

Now past the pandemic, we are starting to hear about concepts like "pandemic fatigue" and "Zoom fatigue." People are so tired of not getting together in person, not having that daily interaction with others and staring into a screen is causing our beloved employees to look and act ghostly!

If you look around the virtual Zoom room and see zombies on your staff, it is time to take stock of your current company culture. The pandemic strained relationships; when your people are looking ghostly, check in on them more often.

Now that some of the daily adjustments to the workplace have been made, take the time to address the humanity of your employees. Start your department meeting with updates from your people, professionally and personally. Encourage your people to take time off, to log off at a reasonable time at night, and take care of themselves. A virtual happy hour is definitely better than nothing. A little appreciation in these trying times will go a long way toward employee health and well-being. And yours too!

And if that doesn't work, try chocolate—the real stuff, not virtual!

Power Thought
Chocolate makes the world go round,
and so do personal relationships.

Day 61:
Why You Need Good Foot Awareness

Katy and I were watching the Broncos beat the Jets. In the middle of the game, we watched a wide receiver make a very difficult catch and drag his toes to make sure that he stayed inbounds. If he hadn't dragged his toes, the catch would have been incomplete.

"He has great foot awareness!" Katy exclaimed.

That comment got me thinking ... How would you recruit for a wide receiver with great foot awareness?

First of all, just being aware that you must have great foot awareness in your new and improved wide receiver is imperative. You can't have what you want unless you know what it is. If you don't know what you want, you can easily drop the ball when hiring.

Second, make sure that you add foot awareness to your Ideal List of things that you must have in your new hire. You don't want another incomplete pass! Coming up with a solid play book that is written down is essential to your success.

Finally, clearly communicate what you are looking for to as many people as you possibly can. Get the message out there, so that your fans can fully support you in your efforts and cheer you on.

Please keep in mind that solid foot awareness is important, but it is equally important that you find someone who fits in with the team culture. At Boise State, they look for "OKG's" which stands for: our kind of guys. The culture fit increases your wide receiver's chance of success on your team.

When you combine skills and culture fit into your hiring strategy, you are guaranteed a winner.

And everyone wants to be a member of a winning team.

Go team go!

Power Thought

Both you and your next hire need
to have great "foot awareness."

Day 62:
Is Your Recruiting in the Toilet?

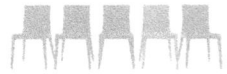

For the past few years, every time I went into my bathroom, I would think, *I need a new toilet seat.* I never did anything about it, because who wants to buy a new toilet seat? I can think of so many other things to spend my money and time on, so I just made do. Even though, my cheap plastic toilet seat would wobble, I would grumble but do nothing. My stupid toilet seat made noise, and I would sigh. I would stare at it in disgust, but still did nothing.

Until one day, it broke completely, and I was forced to buy a new one.

I bought the most expensive toilet seat I could find: It is wood, with a lid that slowly closes. It is solid and it doesn't creak! I installed it myself, and I am inordinately proud of my new toilet seat! Maybe this seems a bit silly, but it really does make a difference in the quality of my daily life, so it feels like a huge accomplishment!

■　　■　　■　　■　　■

Does your recruiting strategy make you grumble? Is your process in the crapper?

Urine luck! (Wink, wink)

My clients are often in the same boat when it comes to recruiting new employees. Like the toilet seat, it doesn't seem like recruiting makes that much difference to the overall company and daily work life. A lot of companies ignore it, even though it stinks, until it breaks so badly that they don't have a choice but to address it.

Updating your recruiting efforts is a great way to improve your candidate pool and your ability to hire great people. Will this make a huge difference in your daily life as a result? You better believe it!

Power Thought

Don't let your recruiting practices fall into the crapper;
replace and redo what you need to!

Day 63:
So ... How Are You?

My friend/colleague, Beth Boen, is the owner of SHE Leads Group, a business networking group for women business owners. A few weeks ago, Beth called me out of the blue. She does this approximately once a year, and asks one simple question:

"How are you?"

She has no other agenda.

I always love our conversations. We talk about business, our families, what is going on with our kids ... And every time I get off the phone with her, I think, *"I am going to do more of this. I am going to reach out to others like Beth does to me."*

■　■　■　■　■

As it turns out, "water cooler" talk helps make employees feel more connected to their co-workers and executives, according to the Denver Business Journal.[1] These conversations connect employees, and really do affect their well-being at work. "Water cooler" talk can bridge the gap, so that controversial topics are easier to work through.

Think about it: When you have a connection to someone, the hard conversation can be easier and the outcomes more innovative. The folks that are more successful at work are ones that engage and connect with each other.

If I'm honest with myself, I know that Beth and I have a strong connection, because she reaches out to me every year. And let's be clear: She is the one that has reached out to me, and it always makes me have a better day.

---

1   https://www.bizjournals.com/bizwomen/news/latest-news/2020/06/missing-office-small-talk-researchers-say-it-impa.html

Let's all make a commitment to engage in more meaningful conversation like Beth Boen, starting now. I challenge you to make two calls a day for the next four days, then see how you feel about the state of the world.

I'll start.

Power Thought

Relationships make the world go round,
and they can start with a simple phone call.

Day 64:
Mr. Right vs. Mr. Right Now

I will never forget the first 70-degree day that I had at my former restaurant, La Iguana. I had owned the place for just a few months, and I had the largest patio in town. When the weather turned just right on a random February day, I drove to work just in time to see a line of people forming out the door and around the block. My stomach dropped to my feet. I didn't have enough food, enough drinks, enough staff, enough cash to make change in the drawers and there was a light bulb out in the women's bathroom.

I called every staff member I had. I barked at them to get their butts over to the restaurant and, "Bring your friends!" If their friend had a pulse and fogged up a mirror, I put them to work. I had no processes, no policies, no procedures, no formal way of doing anything ... and who in the hell was responsible for that burnt out light in the women's bathroom?

Why am I telling you all this?

Because sometimes, you just have to hire Mr. Right Now. You need some temporary help to get you through the uptick in business.

That first year in business wasn't a complete disaster, but it was close. As much business as the restaurant had, I still bled money. Most people that I hired didn't last long, but I got through it. And then I got smart and organized.

■　　■　　■　　■　　■

If you are frantic, with more workload than you can handle, hire Mr. Right Now. Just know the hiring is temporary, because the skillset that you need when you are crazy busy, is not the skillset that you need when things are running more smoothly. Get through today, and then focus on hiring Mr. Right for the long term.

And check to make sure the lightbulb is working in the women's bathroom.

Power Thought

Hire for the short term but keep looking for those
who will be with you for the long term.

Day 65:
How I Got a Killer Tan During COVID

I have a killer tan. I am especially proud of it this year, because the world is in collusion for me to *not* have a tan. I have been to three different beaches on the east and west coast and all were in some sort of closure. "You can't sit here ma'am." "You can only walk on the beach ma'am."

Ugh.

In addition, my neighborhood pool is closed. No water in the pool, and all of the lounge chairs still stacked up neatly along the fence … except for one lonely lounge chair sitting by itself, facing the sun, with the best side table right next to it. I must confess that I've snuck into the pool area several times a week and sat next to the waterless hole in the ground, enjoying the sun.

Not much of a summer vacation.

Or is it?

■　■　■　■　■

We Americans are terrible at resting! We have a built in I-must-appear-busy-to-the-world! attitude that doesn't serve us long-term as Fast Company online notes.[1]

Taking pockets of time to rest and play is equally as important as working hard. You don't have to take an exotic vacation to rest and feel rejuvenated. Take a drive. Walk your neighborhood and pretend that you have never been there before. What or who do you see? Sit on your patio and yell across the street to your neighbor. Unplug.

---

[1]   https://www.fastcompany.com/90515476/how-to-build-a-rest-ethic-that-is-as-strong-as-your-work-one, John Fitch and Max Frenzel, June 6, 2020, accessed July 1, 2023.

Or you can sneak into your neighborhood water-less pool and work on your tan.

And it is a great tan!

Power Thought

Work hard, play hard; that is the American way.

Day 66:
An Act of Bravery During COVID

I made a job offer for one of my clients, and all of us on the hiring committee were all really excited about this candidate. The way he presented himself in the interview process, his references, homework and answers to our questions earned him a job offer. We were thrilled.

Imagine our shock when he turned us down.

"Can we ask why?" said my client.

"You know, I have the opportunity to pursue my dream job, which is in a completely different industry, and I am going to go for it. I really appreciate you, your time and the offer. I will never have this opportunity again, and I am going all in," replied the candidate.

Wow.

There is so much uncertainly in the world. There is so much fear. Watching someone take a leap of faith, despite of all the gloom and doom, is so damn inspiring.

While I am disappointed that I didn't fill the job, and disappointed for my clients who have to keep searching, I am so dang proud of this guy! What an act of bravery!

What brave act are you going to do this week?

Power Thought
Going for the gusto is much more fulling
than settling for the status quo.

Day 67:
Searching for "The One"

When Katy was looking for colleges, she started out with one college in mind, and she didn't want to apply to any others. She was convinced that The University of Texas was the only school for her, and it didn't help that I am a fourth generation University of Texas graduate. I had been indoctrinating her with Longhorn ideas, spirit and paraphernalia since before she was born. Even though I would have loved for her to go to UT, I still thought that applying to just one school seemed very restrictive and short-sighted. She and I fought bitterly, until the day we met Ms. Shelly.

Shelly Humbach of Humbach Education Consulting is a college consultant who helps families like ours. Shelly speaks "teen" and she bridges the gap between Teen Wants and Parent Expectations. She agreed with me that applying to one school was restrictive, but she didn't agree that the University of Texas was all that wonderful.

"They are very stingy with their money!" she said.

Shelly led Katy through a Discovery Process that included an ideal list: What did Katy want from her college experience? What did she want to study? And what kind of climate did Katy like? (She is cold when it is 70 degrees out!). The two of them created a vision for Katy's ideal college experience, narrowed the list down to the top five, then sent us off the visit the campuses. Wouldn't you know? UT did not make the cut.

▪ ▪ ▪ ▪ ▪

Does this process sound familiar to you, my loyal readers? It should!

Countless times, I have been brought into a company where the C-suite is arguing bitterly over a potential hire. They all have great ideas, but they can't agree on how that vision should play out. I always begin with a Discovery Meeting about what they want and need, the vision for the role, and how that role will contribute to the goals of the organization. Often, I am the one that helps bridge the gap for the interview team; after all, I have a 91 percent retention rate for employees after a year.

Katy will be a sophomore at the University of Miami in Miami, Florida, and that school is perfect for her! She loves the size, the location, the climate, the people, the curriculum. It has direct entry nursing, small classes, and she can converse in Spanish with her Uber drivers! The university president is an expert in infectious diseases, and they rolled out their Pandemic plan, so that everyone would be kept as safe as possible. The plan has been a template for other colleges to implement, just another sign that we chose the right place for us. And yet, Katy would never have looked at this school if it hadn't been for Ms. Shelly.

We held out until we found the right fit. We never settled for second choice, and the outcome was beyond awesome.

I advise my clients to do just the same; finding the right employee for the right position saves everyone involved a lot of time, heartache and headaches too. The right fit will change your life.

As for Shelly? She has forever earned a spot on my team of colleagues.

Power Thought

Having someone from outside of your management
team helping guide you through your hiring process
will lead to long term success.

Day 68:
Surgeon #8

As you all know, Katy had a hip replacement, and the recovery went very well.

However, the story I want to tell you is about how she found her surgeon.

When Katy's primary care physician told us that hip surgery would most likely be required for Katy, she also recommended that Katy get a second opinion. We found the first surgeon through a referral. He confirmed that she would have to have a replacement, but he didn't perform that type of surgery.

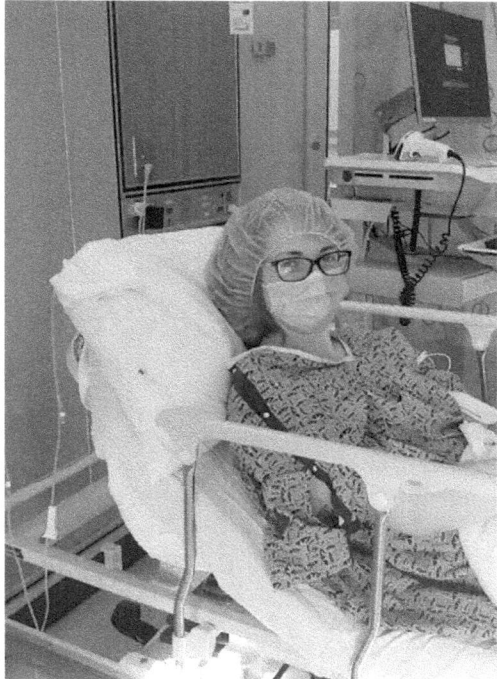

We made an appointment with Surgeon #2. When we arrived at his office, they had no record of her having an appointment. We were told that we could reschedule in eight weeks.

Surgeon #3: We were told to go to one location by a scheduler. When we arrived, we were told that the doctor didn't work at that location on that day, but we could call back and re-schedule for four-to-five weeks out.

Katy called four more surgeons. Three never called her back, and one called back but had no openings.

(Does this sound like your hiring process?)

Finally, Katy called Surgeon #8, Dr. Nicholas Ting. He had a cancellation the next day at 2:45. Would we like to come in? Why, yes. Yes, we would.

Dr. Ting was on time. He was kind, thorough, patient and knowledgeable. He called Katy by name and asked her about her college classes. He answered all of her questions, and though I am positive he has a very tight schedule, Katy felt like he had all day for her. He had a text message service that provided updates and tips on a great recovery.

On the day of the surgery, Dr. Ting came to visit Katy beforehand. He explained how everything would go. He came to the waiting room to talk with me after the surgery was over. He visited Katy at the hospital at 7:30 p.m. that night to see how she was, and five days post-surgery he personally called her to check in.

Katy has had five surgeries. He was by far the single best doctor we have ever encountered.

■ ■ ■ ■ ■

Waiting for the right candidate to come along takes patience and discipline. It isn't easy. You think it is never going to happen. But, if you wait, that person will walk into your life and change it. I promise.

Power Thought

Patience is a virtue and having patience (patients!)
will help you make the right hire at the right time.

Day 69:
How You Hire a Fritzy

Katy and I foster dogs, and one dog was a part cattle dog named Fritzy. She loved to tree squirrels! She would make a beeline to any squirrel within a three-mile radius. It was horrible to take her on walks, because all she wanted to do was tree squirrels. We tried every trick in the book to get her to not tree squirrels, to no avail.

My most worrisome thought was, *Who is going to adopt Fritzy?* All she wants to do is chase squirrels, so she won't be good for just any family. They will have to have some property for her to run around and do her thing, or it would never work out.

■　■　■　■　■

Every time I meet with a new client, they always say to me, "I have this very unique position, and it will take a very special person with the right kind of skill-set in order to be the right hire. How will I ever find this person?"

You start with a vision for this individual.

On Fritzy's profile, I listed: "High-energy dog who is a champion squirrel chaser. If you have a rodent problem, Fritzy is the dog for you!"

When hiring, if you need an engineer who is also a people person, list that in your ad. If you need a wholesale buyer who can also sell parts, write that down. You can't have what you want unless you ask for it.

And for Fritzy? I took her to an adoption event, and a family walked up to me asking, "Where is the Champion Squirrel Chaser?"

I said, "Are you joking?"

They replied, "No! We have a chicken farm, and we need a dog who will chase squirrels and rats."

I am happy to report that Fritzy cleared out the rodent problem at the chicken farm in less than two weeks. The family loves her, and she runs all over the farm all day every day. She has never been happier.

Power Thought

You may have a unique hiring situation,
but there is a unique hire waiting for you.

Day 70:
How You Recover from Crappy Circumstances

Katy needed hip surgery, because of an infection years ago the caused her to develop arthritis, and she had very little cartilage left to cushion the joint. Her new titanium hip will restore her body to its youth, and it will allow her pain-free movement once again.

When we first received the news that a hip replacement would be the doctor's recommended course of treatment, I bawled my eyes out. But not Katy. My daughter beamed from ear to ear! When I later asked her why she was so happy, she replied by saying "The worst-case scenario would be them saying there was nothing they could do to help me. They have a plan to fix me."

Katy was able to look at the situation she was given and find the bright side. She was grateful for the opportunity to be treated, and looked at the surgery as a way to better empathize with, and relate to, her future patients once she becomes a nurse.

I think there is a lesson here for all of us to learn. Developing an infection at age seven and needing a hip replacement at age nineteen were circumstances no one could have predicted for my daughter. Instead of dwelling on the odds or the cards dealt, Katy chose to look at what she could learn and be grateful to have found a fix, and an amazing surgeon to help her.

We can't control what happens to us, but we can control how we react to it. With many bumps along the road, the most powerful thing we can do is choose to enjoy the journey with our loved ones.

I am really inspired by my daughter's positive outlook on this whole ordeal, and I carry that forward with me as I navigate my road in life.

I hope that you can too.

Power Thought

Attitude is everything.

Day 71:
Back in the Saddle Again

When I was a little girl, I attended a summer camp in the backwoods of Texas along the Guadalupe River. I learned how to ride horses at that camp, because that is what good Texas girls do!

During one of my very first times on a horse, I quickly turned around to talk to my friend behind me, and I accidentally kicked my horse. (When you gently kick your horse, you are telling the horse to go.) He started to move forward, and I fell off the back.

I got up, bruised and dirty, dusted myself off, and started walking toward the gate to leave. My instructor called out, "Where are you going? You gotta get back in that saddle!"

Oh, no. No way! No how! I had already decided my horseback riding career was over.

It took much convincing and bargaining for my instructor to get me back on that horse. She said, "The longer you stay off the horse after a fall, the harder it is to get back up on it. It is scary, you are rattled. Don't let that prevent you from trying again."

■   ■   ■   ■   ■

We've all been knocked off our horses. The times we live in can feel scary and we can feel totally rattled. But we can all look at ways to "get back on the horse."

When hiring, this looks like: Calling that client. Writing that blog. Sending a thank you to your favorite vendor. Take that one action that you have been putting off in order to get going again.

I did get back up on that horse, and boy am I glad I did! I won an award in the final summer rodeo, but I also learned a tremendous life lesson.

Get back in the saddle people! It's time to ride. Yeehaw!

Day 72:
How to Manage Remote Workers

When I bought my restaurant, the first problem I had to solve was how to manage workers that worked opposite hours from me. By the time my night staff left the bar at 3:30–4:00 a.m. my janitorial staff was usually arriving to get the place clean for the next day. This meant that I had someone in my building for whom I was responsible almost 24 hours a day, 7 days a week.

So, how do you manage people that you never see? This question is being asked by almost every business these days, and many have not faced this issue before.

Here are some tips:

- Start your day with a fifteen-minute virtual team huddle. Have everyone give you their top two priorities for the day and something that they are grateful for. Ask them what they need from you that day, and then provide it. Have a longer meeting once a week to follow up and provide guidance.

- Ask questions. For example, if someone approaches you with a problem, ask, "What do you think we need to do about that?" Or, "How would you solve that problem?" Remember: they know more about their job than you do, so solicit their input.

- Focus on *why* not *how*. Give your team the reason *why* you are working on a particular project instead of directions on *how* to get it done. Let them take the ball and run with it.

- Give parameters. I used to say to my managers, "If you can justify your decision based on our core values, then I will back you up 100 percent." This gives your team room to expand and innovate. They need to know that you have their back.

- Finally, don't make excuses for people who aren't performing. Everyone gets frazzled and discombobulated, and are juggling more than usual, but your top performers are still getting the work done. If you have someone who isn't, make the hard call on behalf of the rest of the team.

The biggest breakthrough that I had about managing a remote team of top performers is that I needed to trust them to do their work and do it well. Maybe they didn't do it the way that I would have, but if the outcome is the same or better, what difference does it make?

■　■　■　■　■

I recently had a Zoom call with several of the people that had worked for me, and they are all in high-powered jobs and leaders in their organizations. I am convinced their success, beyond working for me, lies in the fact that I literally could not micro-manage them. I had to trust and have faith that the job would get done. And you know what? It did.

Happy Leading Remote Teams!

Power Thought
Trusting people until they show you
not to is the best path to take.

Day 73:
How to Lead Well When You Are Afraid

I have had a few conversations with clients who really want to do right by their people. However, they are justifiably stressed and concerned. As one person asked me, "How do I lead people through fear when I am afraid, too?"

Here is the plan that we created.

Step 1: *Breathe like this:* Take two minutes. Breathe in for a count of five, and breathe out for ten. Do this for two minutes. What this does is get the oxygen all the way through your lungs and when you flood the body with oxygen, you think more clearly. Out with the old and in with the new.

Step 2: *Prioritize exercise:* Even if you walk briskly through your neighborhood for twenty minutes, exercise is key to your mental health. By getting some sunshine, pumping some Vitamin D through your veins along with oxygenated blood, your thoughts become are clearer, and you can communicate better with your team.

Step 3: *Focus on gratitude:* What are you grateful for? Are you grateful that you found toilet paper at the grocery store? Are you grateful that the Himalayan mountains are being seen for the first time in thirty years? Are you grateful that you get to spend more time with your kids (even when they frustrate you)? Are you grateful that the sun is shining? Whatever it is, focus on that. The body is flooded with feel-good hormones when you focus on gratitude, which also helps you think clearly, and from a positive place rather than a negative one. Then, lead your team through a gratitude exercise. They need it, too.

Step 4: *Take one day at a time:* For most of my clients who are truly visionary, and live in and for the future, this is probably the hardest step. Things are changing so rapidly, and the world feels so uncertain now that making future plans can be very scary. So, focus on *today*. Do great work *today*. Take care of your clients *today*. Then, put it away, and hug your loved ones.

We can and will get through it together. And, if you need more support, please call me. My phone line is open and available to anyone.

You got this.

Power Thought

Make the phrase "do it afraid" a mantra your life.

Day 74:
From Crisis Comes Opportunity

In 2006, I had gotten out of the restaurant business, and I took a year off to figure out what I wanted to do next. Katy had just started kindergarten, and I had this "free time." But I was also totally stressed out. I needed to make money. I was afraid of the future. And I was experiencing a crisis! Even though I watched a lot of Law and Order and played free cell constantly, I was so bored! Then, one day, I woke up in the middle of the night, and I knew that I needed to start A-list.

After my business was established, I was talking to my speech coach, Margaret Romney, about the fears that my clients have about the future. She then said to me, "Do you know what the criteria is for a crisis?"

My response: "There is criteria for a crisis?"

"Yes. There are five."

According to *Effective Crisis Communication* by Ulmer, Sellnow and Seeger, they are:[1]

- It is unexpected
- It disrupts routine
- It produces uncertainty
- It is a threat
- It creates opportunity

Check out number five. As soon as I heard that, I thought, *no wonder we have such mixed feelings about a crisis; there is opportunity in the middle of this mess!*

During the COVID crisis, once again I watched a lot of Law and Order and played free cell. But I also worked closely with my clients, wrote

---

[1] "Effective Crisis Communication: Moving From Crisis to Opportunity" Fifth Edition, Robert R. Ulmer, Timothy L. Sellnow, and Matthew W. Seeger, September 2022 SAGE Publications, Inc.

my second book, worked on my speech writing *and* worked on a video series. I have also created my next business opportunity.

I have done it before, and will do it again.

And, so can you. Focus and create!

Power Thought

Every crisis presents an opportunity … if you look for it.

Day 75:
Hiring in Uncertain Times

I got a call from a client who said, "Beth, it seems ridiculous to be hiring during all of this uncertainty, but I still need this position filled, and I need it filled with the right fit. Let's keep going."

Like some of you, I have owned my businesses during 9/11, during the Recession of 2008–2009, and through COVID-19. And through all this uncertainty, the same question keeps coming up over and over: Should I move forward with hiring?

Here are some things you should consider when making a decision.

- *Hire what you need today.* Many of my clients are true visionaries, and their gift is to think long term rather than immediate. What I mean is, they are thinking five years down the road. For example: "If I hire this Social Media Coordinator, they can become my VP of Marketing in five years." That may or may not be true, but it doesn't matter in the moment. What you need *today* is a Social Media Coordinator. Focus on that.

- *Go back to basics.* While you have downtime, focus on where your company isn't doing well during the good times. Maybe your follow-through with clients isn't speedy enough. Maybe there is a gap in your sales pipeline. Maybe production is slower than it should be. The economy will come back; it always does. When the boom comes, do you have the right people in the right seats on the bus? Is your infrastructure in place? Take some time to really think this through, and it will help you decide if hiring is necessary and prudent right now.

- *Trust your gut.* Crazy or not, when you need a position filled, you need it filled with the right person. Make sure that your interview process is solid enough to hire the right person the first time. And, if you need this position filled today, then move forward confidently.

There is no doubt that hiring during uncertain times is a leap of faith. It is a step into the unknown, which can be scary and exhilarating at the same time. When you are ready to take the leap, then let's take it together.

Power Thought

A leap of faith is necessary, in good times and bad.

Day 76:
How You Evaluate a Freudian Slip?

There is so much pressure in a job interview: The employer wants to fill a position and the potential employee wants a job! Because of this high intensity, people are prone to saying the oddest things. If you are the person doing the hiring, how do you objectively evaluate the potential candidate to determine if nerves are at play, or if there is truly an issue worth examining?

Take this example from an actual interview: "I am an alcoholic. I mean, workaholic."

Many people doing the hiring would assume the candidate was joking and ignore a comment like this; perhaps even chalk it up to interview nerves. Some people would laugh it off and maybe follow up with something like, "Ha! Ha! I am, too! Workaholic, I mean!" (Wink, wink, nudge nudge.)

In this particular interview, however, the Freudian slip coupled with additional red flags gave my client pause. The candidate's speech was slurred, they complained about their past boss having an alcohol problem, and they also pointed out that their counterpart was fired for drinking on the job.

So how do you evaluate a candidate like this one?

If all evidence is telling you that it wasn't a Freudian slip, think about the potential risk this person brings to you and your company. There is a theme in this interview that has nothing to do with the job at hand, so it likely isn't just a slip, or nerves talking. At the end of the day, your gut knows best, and moving along to the next candidate is probably the wisest course of action.

Power Thought
We all have the gift of intuition,
and it is up to us to use it.

Day 77:
Do You Know What Your Candidates Want More Than Anything?

When Katy was in her second semester of her freshmen year at the University of Miami, she decided to go through rush for a sorority. Each sorority had a sales pitch, goodie bags and t-shirts to offer, in addition to scholarship and job opportunities during and after college. After a full week of parties, get-togethers, meetings at all hours of the day and night and inspiring speeches, she called me on the verge of tears. "Mom, I just wish I had some answers!"

That got me thinking: The same goes for hiring candidates. You can offer people big salaries, benefits galore, pool tables and dry-cleaning services, but all of that is meaningless if they don't get a solid, meaningful job offer. What candidates really want are answers. Timely, relevant, definitive answers. After all, they are making a decision that will significantly affect their life.

Case in point: A candidate called me to say thank you. He said the A-list Interviews process was the most transparent and informative job-seeking process he had ever been through. "Just knowing when I would have an answer really reduced my stress, and I just wanted to say thank you for communicating with me clearly through a very difficult time," he added.

This voicemail came *after* we chose a different candidate for the position he was seeking.

If you want to attract and retain great employees, start treating them well from the very instant they send you a resume. Communicate when they will have answers and meet those deadlines. Treating people like people goes a long way; it gives them positive feeling, and a sense they will be treated well as an employee too.

As for my kid? She pledged AD Phi and couldn't be happier.

Power Thought

Clear communication and timely
answers benefit everyone.

Day 78:
Are Your Employees Disengaged?
Do This.

If you are frustrated with employees who are disengaged and not producing at a high level, you are not alone. There have been several studies recently about the number of disengaged employees at work and how much distraction it causes which leads to the question: What can employers and managers do to change the level of engagement at work?[1]

First things first: Watch your language. Stop referring to your employees as: Head count. Butts in seats. Bodies. Staff. Talent. All these words are degrading, and not designed to create solid working relationships, or make employees feel valued in their positions.

Instead, say this: My team. My village. My tribe. My community. My connections. My people. My colleagues.

Do you *hear* the difference? Do *you* see the difference?

When you engage with your people and make them feel as important as they truly are to your organization, they will engage with you, their leader. It's astonishing what a small shift in language, and perhaps even mindset, can do for a company.

Happy hiring, my people!

Power Thought

People are human "beings" not human "doings."

---

1   https://www.achievers.com/press/achievers-survey-finds-that-despite-disengagement-65-of-employees-plan-to-stay-in-their-jobs/

Day 79:
Why Your Outbound Recruiting Efforts Don't Work

I recently attended the Indeed.com Academy to become a better recruiter, and boy, did I learn a ton!

First, the basics. There are two different types of recruiting: inbound and outbound. Inbound is when an employer places an ad on a website and the applications start coming in. Outbound is when an internal recruiter sifts through resumes, picks up the phone and calls the candidate to invite them to interview for a position.

While this concept isn't new, the research behind it is. If a recruiter calls a candidate who didn't submit a resume for the job, it costs the employer significantly more money, more time and results in less success. A person who submits a resume of their own volition is infinitely better every time.

The question is why?

Here's the bottom line: There is a mental process that a candidate must go through in order to begin looking for a job. They must come to the realization that their current job isn't going to work out, they must realize that things aren't going to get any better, and, most importantly, that they must make a change to a different company. If your candidate hasn't made that mental shift, your recruiting efforts cost more time, effort, and money.

Instead of focusing on outbound recruiting, focus your efforts on your inbound recruiting. Spend time to key word your ad properly, create your Ideal list and don't forget to listen, listen, listen. In the long run, you'll be glad that you did.

Power Thought

Inbound candidates are statistically
way more successful.

Day 80:
If You Just Fired Someone, *Don't* Do This

Firing someone, even if it is the best thing for all parties, is awful. It feels terrible. Even if you knew it was coming, and even if it wasn't a surprise to your employee, it still feels totally horrendous. You have a pit in your stomach, and your overall feeling is enough to make you want to hire someone as fast as you possibly can to fill that hole.

Don't.

"Why not?" You ask. "I need to fill this seat asap!"

When you hire from a panic place, rather than a place of reason and overall calm, that is when you make hiring mistakes.

According to Robert Plotkin, who wrote "How to Prevent Internal Bar Theft".[1]

> "Hiring the wrong bartender can be staggering. It's better to operate short-handed for a period of time and rely on your existing staff to cover the bar than hiring someone unqualified or inappropriate for the establishment. It will be more advantageous in the long-run to delay hiring another bartender until the right candidate can be found."

In addition, Warren Buffet says, "Money flows from the impatient to the patient." I believe this to be true in any area of life. In any situation where big decisions must be made, we all operate and make decisions better from a place of measured calm than from panicked overthinking.

When you have the unfortunate experience of firing someone, I want you to pause. Take a big, deep breath. Let the emotions settle down. Call a team meeting and rally the troops. Let everyone know that it will be okay, and that you are committed to hiring the very best candidate you possibly can. And, then wait at least two weeks before you do anything.

---

1   "Preventing Internal Theft: A Bar Owner's Guide" Robert Plotkin, Published by Barmedia, 1998, pg. 86.

Our instinct as humans is to replace a person in our lives as fast as we possibly can. In the end, learning why that person no longer serves you and your organization is the better path, and proceeding from a place of calm will serve you best in the end.

Power Thought

Slowing down your hiring process will
save you money in the long run.

Day 81:
What to Do with an Entitled Employee

I had a potential client call me frustrated with an employee. She said, "I just gave out bonuses, and she wants more money ... I don't know what to do!"

Having seemingly entitled employees is a hot topic of conversation these days. Here is my thought: *An entitled employee is in the wrong job.*

Think about it.

When an employee is in a job that they love, they are happy. They think about the work that they "get to do," not what they "have to do." They may ask for a raise or for more vacation time, but rarely are these on the forefront of their minds. They are excited to work every day because they are passionate about their objectives. They feel confident and are thriving.

But when they are not happy in their jobs? They will do anything to keep themselves engaged. They think that money will make them happy. They think that more time off will make them happy. Or free movie tickets, a gift certificate for a massage or getting to work from home. But in the end, if they are not enjoying their jobs anymore, have a conversation with these employees about doing something else within the company ... or you will have to let them go.

Nothing can make up for doing work that they do not enjoy, and I do mean nothing!

When you have an entitled employee, don't talk about more money, benefits, working from home, etc.; it won't help, and it only increases frustration for both you and your employee. Instead, talk about the job duties, and ask if this is really the work they love. If it's not? Either move them to a position that is right for them or help them transition out gracefully.

Remember: You as the employer are entitled to an employee who wants to do the job you are offering.

Power Thought

Entitlement equates to unhappiness.

I had lunch with a retired consultant who had been a big wig at Sears in the 1980s. Back then, Sears was in its hey-day and was worth about $6 billion as a company. I asked this gentleman what he thought made them so successful. His response really surprised me: "The CEO had a full time 'Atta-Boy' Girl."

Ummm ... what?

The CEO at the time instructed his personal assistant to start looking for people in the company who had done good work, because he wanted to promote great customer service in Sears. She began soliciting stories of people who had gone above and beyond the standard to provide great customer service. The CEO would then write a personalized, hand-written thank you note. Eventually her role as the Atta-Boy Girl became a full-time job. She would hear about these stories, type up the note, and every day at 4:30, she would take these letters to the CEO; he would read them, sign his name to them, and she would send them out.

Can you imagine what commitment it took for him to do that? Can you imagine what impact that made? Sears ultimately replaced that CEO with another who was not committed to the thank you letter writing campaign, and the company is currently closing its last remaining stores. Coincidence?

If you want to improve your company culture, start with a simple thank you, and grow it to needing a full-time Atta Boy Girl/Atta Girl Boy/whatever.

There is quite simply no better use of your time.

Power Thought

Success rides on recognizing the value
and contributions of others.

Day 83:
What the Pay Gap Really Means to You

Michelle Williams has unwittingly become *the* spokesperson for the pay gap in Hollywood. She drew attention to this gap in 2018, when the media revealed that she was paid a mere $1,000 for re-shooting scenes in a Ridley Scott movie in comparison to Mark Wahlberg, who made $1.5 million for the same work. In her brilliant speech at the Emmys, Williams stated that, "When you put value into a person, it empowers that person to get in touch with their own inherent value. And where do they put that value? They put it into their work."[1]

It seems impossible for one person to make such a large impact in the workplace, particularly in a company or industry culture that has gender or race pay gaps ingrained deeply within. Michelle Williams used her speech as a forum to do just that, and boy was it amazing!

■ ■ ■ ■ ■

As a female entrepreneur, who has dedicated her career to placing people in work that they love and all that entails, I could not agree more. Creating a culture of empowerment, value and equality does in fact change the world. Employees spend a significant amount of their time in the workplace. By creating a place of value, harmony and equality, you promote this, not only at work, but in the world beyond. Valued people spread value in the world, and as a benefit to employers, they become more valuable workers.

Be the employer who can proudly say you value your employees and their worth as human beings, regardless of what larger culture may accept or allow.

---

1   https://www.bing.com/videos/search?q=Michelle+Wiliams+equal+pay+speech&qpvt= Michelle+Wiliams+equal+pay+speech&view=detail&mid=C6836862D56BE78F90A1C6 836862D56BE78F90A1&&FORM=VRDGAR&ru=%2Fvideos%2Fsearch%3Fq%3DMichelle %2BWiliams%2Bequal%2Bpay%2Bspeech%26qpvt%3DMichelle%2BWiliams%2Bequal %2Bpay%2Bspeech%26FORM%3DVDVRE

Power Thought

Focus on narrowing the gap between
who people are and what they do.

Day 84:
Do You Have Zombies in the Workplace?

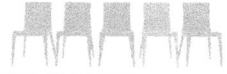

Do you walk into your office and see Zombies disguised as employees? Those lifeless bodies that wander around thoughtlessly in packs? Have you ever thought about how they got that way?

New employees are so always excited to start their new job. I have heard many new hires talk about their first day on the job just like they talk about their first day of school... with excitement and a lot of awe. So how is it that years or even months into their employment with a company, they lose their passion for the job?

Because we suck the life out of them with too many constraints and not enough direction. We make it hard for them to do their jobs with petty rules. We don't spend enough time training our new people, and we really don't take the time to explain our expectations to them. All of the sudden, we have a lifeless body of the previously excited employee.

If you look around and see zombies on your staff, it is time to take stock in your interviewing process, your training program and your employee handbook. If you are dictating when someone can go to the bathroom, you are running a daycare, not a professional office. It is time for a re-do.

And if that doesn't work, try chocolate.

Power Thought
Don't turn your employees into zombies
with too many restrictions!

Day 85:
It's STILL Cheesy!

I have a client who asks candidates this question: "If you were a type of cheese, which would it be?" The question makes people laugh and we have had some pretty clever responses. "Pepper Jack: I'm spicy!" and, "Any one of them except blue cheese, because that one stinks!" are among a few of the responses I've heard so far.

For a cheese maker, a chef and perhaps a dairy farmer, this question might be appropriate. Perhaps, even a marketing position could warrant this question, as you might be measuring a person's creativity.

However, for most industries and positions, the information you are getting by asking that question is like just like Swiss cheese—full of holes. How does a description of cheese really evaluate the candidate's qualities, integrity, and passion for their work? Would you eliminate them from your candidate pool, if they described themselves as Velveeta?

Focus on asking measurable questions in your interview and truly listen to your candidates. It is really the best way to get the relevant information that you need. Anything else is, well... cheesy

Power Thought

Cheese is best left as an appetizer for dinner guests,
and should not be part of your hiring process.

Day 86:
How Humanity Holds You Back from Hiring the Right Person

When interviewing people for jobs, one of the most common problems that my clients have is they "feel sorry" for the candidates. "I just want to offer the job to all of them!"

I often ask, "Do you know why you want to offer the job to all the people?"

Most people have no idea why they struggle, but the answer is simple: We are biologically wired to include others. We are biologically wired for connection. So, when someone comes in for an interview, and they are nervous, anxious, worried and scared, we want to make it better. We want to help them feel better, and help them succeed in the interview.

Here is the disconnect. When you have 300 applicants and one job, you will reject at least 299 of your candidates. You may reject all 300, re-post the ad, and keep going. And it is difficult, because we aren't wired to reject people. You have to be exclusionary when you are hiring, which goes against our humanity and our most basic instincts as humans.

So next time that you are hiring someone, remind yourself of this: instead of "rejecting" someone, you are releasing them into the universe so that they can find their dream job and you can find your dream candidate. It's a win/win.

Everyone deserves to be happy, especially you. Don't forget that next time you endeavor to hire someone.

Power Thought
Rejection is protection.

Day 87:
When You Need to Hire Fast

Last week I had a client call me in a panic. He was about to lose a large government contract, because he hadn't hired a much-needed engineer. We were in the process of filling the position, but we weren't moving fast enough for the government.

Now I have heard it all!

If you know me and my hiring philosophy, you know that I am not an advocate for fast hires. I believe very strongly that hiring fast means you will hire wrong. It is so easy to make mistakes when you move too quickly, and, as Robert Plotkin states in his book *Preventing Internal Theft*, "It's better to operate short-staffed for a period of time and rely on your existing staff than hiring someone unqualified or inappropriate for the establishment."[1]

However, no rule is correct or applicable 100 percent of the time. When you are in the situation my client found himself in, and you are faced with losing a few million dollars in government contracts, you need to hire fast. My advice for this situation was hire someone quickly, get the position filled, *and* continue to look for the right fit. If the quick-hire person works out—and it does about one-third of the time—then wonderful. Everyone is happy. If they don't work out, remember this was a short-term solution, and be grateful for that.

Power Thought
Hire fast when absolutely necessary.
Hire right for long-term success.

---

1   "Preventing Internal Theft: A Bar Owner's Guide" Robert Plotkin, Published by Barmedia, 1998.

Day 88:
A Second-Generation Killer Tan!

When I took two weeks off work to move Katy to college, I knew how important it was for me to be there with her to start of her journey, which brings up an important topic that I preach to my clients often: Everyone needs time away from work, whether it be for important milestones in their personal lives, or for a vacation that allows them time to rejuvenate, recuperate and come back to work in a better place!

The fact remains that everyone needs time away from work, even when you own the company, like me. Some of my clients get really excited when a candidate tells us in an interview that they *never* take vacations. I actually think this is a negative. Inspiration rarely comes to someone sitting in their office answering emails. Inspiration comes from experiences and usually those come after office hours.

As a nation, we are not good at taking vacation anyway. We feel that we can't get away, we can't unplug or we might miss something. I think we miss things when we don't take time off.

When your employees want to take vacation time, praise them for it. Say thank you. Then ask them what you can do to help facilitate their vacation time so they are not performing work while away. Not only will they think that you are the greatest boss ever, but they will come back recharged, renewed and inspired. Your business will benefit, and therefore, so will you. Maybe then you can take some time off too.

I was grateful that I took the time to be with Katy on her journey to college, and I came back to work ready to tackle work with renewed energy and vision.

Power Thought

"Rest and relax, relax and rest" is a recipe
for greater productivity.

Day 89:
Is Hiring Still a Hardship? Yes, It Is.

I was chosen as a speaker for *Vistage*, an executive coaching organization that helps CEOs and executives of all levels become better leaders.[1] All speakers receive ratings based on content, delivery and real-world applicability. I was honored and humbled to receive 5 out of 5 for content and real-world applicability, and it definitely reaffirmed something that I find in my business each day: Hiring good people for any size organization continues to be relevant, challenging and the defining cornerstone of any organization.

If you are continuing to find this challenge, remember that I'm here to help your organization personally, or to continue to spread the word through speaking engagements. This challenge is here to stay, and I'm ready to help alleviate some of the stress of hiring.

Power Thought
We all need each other, especially in hiring.

---

1   https://www.vistage.com/

Day 90:
Everyone Needs a Corner Man

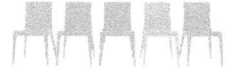

Let's talk about the heavy bag ... the bane of my workout routine.

When I was learning how to box, I had a particularly bad workout with the bleeping heavy bag. I was coming off a week with lots of physical activity, and I hadn't slept well the night before. All in all, the stars aligned for a bad workout, and frustration took over. When things weren't going the way I wanted, I broke down in tears over the $#%@! heavy bag.

My trainer, who is an accomplished boxer himself, pulled me aside and said, "Everyone needs a Corner Man. Someone who is in your corner, pushing you when you need it, giving you water and a towel at the bell, and cheering you on in your hard moments." These words really resonated with me, because I think everyone needs this reminder from time to time—both in business and in life.

■ ■ ■ ■ ■

I have often seen this of level of frustration during the hiring process. A candidate that you thought would be amazing backs out at the last minute. The one applicant that you wanted to hire blows an interview. You have eight interviews scheduled in a day, and no one makes the cut. What most people do in this moment is give up and say, "Just hire someone already!" when this is the time to keep pushing forward. After all, dealing with people is always unpredictable, and situations arise that you don't expect. When hiring, a "Corner Man" knows just when to step in and remind you that *now* is the time to stay strong, because giving up will only lead to more frustration and eventual regret.

If you find yourself completely frustrated with the hiring process, and are ready to throw in the towel, I can help. I would be honored to be your Corner Man, to cheer you on and remind you that the right person is out there if you just keep pushing forward.

In the meantime, I am back on the (damn) heavy bag with my trainer in my corner.

Sincerely,

Your Corner Man (Woman)

Power Thought

When you have a Corner Man, they can help
you through the heaviness of hiring.

Day 91:
Pay Your New Employees to be on Time?

A friend of mine was hired recently to work for a large corporation. Upon being hired, he was informed that if he arrived to work on time for his first two straight weeks, he would receive an $800 bonus. Further, if he arrived on time for the following two straight weeks, he would receive another $800 bonus. Finally, if he was on time for work for four straight weeks, he would receive an additional $2000. Thus, the motivation of the company is a guarantee that any new employee would be on time for work for their first eight weeks, setting good habits for on-time work arrival.

As I have recounted this story to those in my network, the reactions have been varied and intense. Comments such as:

- "You have got to be kidding me! They are paying someone a bonus to show up for work?"

- "Is this what we have come to as to implement company culture?"

- "I thought that being on time for work is what a salary is for."

- "What happened to the work ethic?"

It is interesting to me the visceral reactions to using monetary bonuses to reinforce desired behavior in an employee. It is also very interesting to me as to why the company feels compelled to offer money to an employee to ensure they will be on time.

The real fact is that consistently being late is a sign of lack of commitment. If your new employees are not automatically arriving to work at the agreed upon time, they should not have been hired. Ask more questions during your interviews about timeliness to avoid having to incentivize punctuality. After all, your time is too valuable to invest in a bad hire.

Power Thought

Be careful when incentivizing and know exactly
what and why you are offering any incentives.

Day 92:
Dear Valued Employee:
Click Here to Resign

I have a very good friend that I'll call Charles, who works for a huge global company of around 30,000 employees. Charles has worked for this company for twenty-one years, and recently decided to resign. He felt that he had grown all that he could in his current role, and has chosen to move on.

He dutifully called the HR department to respectfully give his two-week's notice. He was told that in order to resign, he had to go to the company website, find the HR page and click on the link to resign.

It gets better.

Then, he had fourteen days to "change his mind." All he had to do was to go back to the company website, click on the HR page, find his resignation and click cancel.

During that two-week period, no human being reached out to him. No one told his team. There was no one to turn his equipment into. He left with zero fanfare. After twenty-one years.

Please keep in mind that this company will pay $10,000 for any referral that becomes a full-time employee.

And we wonder why employees aren't more fully engaged at work. Perhaps it is time to put the "human" back into HR.

Power Thought

Surely, we can do better than this!

Day 93:
Your Membership to "Bad Hires Anonymous"

I was having a lovely conversation with a potential new vendor. I was telling her about how my bad hire many years ago had made national news, and launched my career as an interviewing coach. I told her this was a club in which no one wanted to be a member. She graciously laughed, then said, "You received a lifetime membership to the BHA: Bad Hires Anonymous."

Boy, did I ever.

All of the clients that I have worked with over the years have been, and are currently, a member of this club. It is almost like you have to be a member before you understand the true devastation of a bad hire.

Please note that you are not alone. Here are the criteria for club membership: Anyone who has been in business for any length of time who has ever hired an employee, and anyone who has been in charge of employees, has at some point made a bad hire.

What I want you to know is that this is not representative of you. A bad hire isn't something to be ashamed of, or something that you need to hide. It is simply an indicator of a skillset that you need to learn and that you ensure that your employees learn.

In the meantime, welcome to the club.

Power Thought

We're in the hiring process together,
and you can learn from my experience.

Day 94:
You Cannot Decide on a Candidate.
Now What?

I was retained to work with a company to hire a vice president for their organization. We developed an ideal candidate list, reviewed the job description, began recruiting and interviewed, until we had narrowed down to a single promising candidate. We have interviewed the woman three times and sent her the job description. She successfully completed a skills assignment and wrote a 30/60/90-day plan, to ensure success for her potential new position. I called references of former bosses, peers and direct reports. After completing the entire interviewing process with this candidate, the only component left was the actual choice to hire or not, and my client could not decide either way. We had an interview team of nine people, who, when asked for their insight, all had differing and conflicting thoughts. As another of my clients once described, "This is muddy data."

What happens when you have completed your entire interviewing system with a candidate, yet still do not feel confident in a choice?

Well, let me make it clear.

If you are truly unable to make a confident hiring decision about an individual, they are not the right person for the position. Simply stated, do not hire them. The cost of training, development and retention of your employees is too large of a risk to take on an uncertain selection. If you are still "not sure" after an intensive and comprehensive interview process, consider the effects of a potential bad hire on your clients, other employees, vendors, and other business partners. The stakes are too high for you to decide on muddy data.

Hiring a new person is a big turning point for you and your company. If you have doubts, return to the beginning of your interviewing process: look at your ideal candidate list again, make sure that the vision for this role is still accurate. Check the job ad and ask yourself, *Did I articulate the vision for this position clearly?* Ultimately, my best advice is to keep looking.

You *will* clear up any questions that you have by holding out for the right fit. When the right person for your company comes along, you will feel as if you have won the lottery. If you do not feel that way, hold out until you do. It will be in everyone's best interest.

Power Thought

Don't hire until the "data" is clear.

Day 95:
The Hot Dog Vendor in the Red-light District

I was working with an up-and-coming technology company that was interviewing for a Vice President, and we flew in a promising candidate to discuss the position further. When asked to describe the best job he had ever had, the client said, "I was a hot dog vendor in the red-light district, and I got to hang out with the ladies of evening." Then he laughed.

This candidate checked off all of our other boxes: He had held the position before in another growing tech firm, he had the leadership skills that we wanted and he was eager to get started, but this comment stopped us in our tracks.

As we discussed the candidate after the interview, one member of the interview team said that the candidate was "just joking" and we shouldn't hold that comment against him.

But what if he wasn't joking? There is a huge potential risk to take on when a candidate alludes to sex in an interview.

The bottom line is this: Referring to and/or alluding to sex in a professional interview is completely inappropriate, no matter what the company, the product, the experience or the position. Whether this candidate meant to or not, you as the employer can't, under any circumstances, take on that risk. It puts all of your other employees in a terrible position, should this candidate not limit his inappropriateness to the interview process.

In other words, we can't assume that he was joking.

Next!

Power Thought
Off-color comments need to be taken seriously.

I love Mexican food. I mean, I really *love* Mexican food! And the spicier the food, the better I like it! The beans and rice with jalapeños, the cheese with green chilis, the sizzling beef with peppers on my plate of fajitas yum. It makes my heart sing!

Whenever there is a new Mexican food restaurant, I am the first to try it. I soak in all the spicy goodness as fast as I can, because, like many Mexican food restaurants, the food profile is going to change ... dang it!

During the first year in business, most restaurants embark with recipes of authentic Mexican flavor and spiciness. Over the course of time, they begin to make the food less spicy, after receiving complaints from people who do not like spicy. (No complaints from Texans, mind you!) The restaurant appeases this small handful of people, rather than standing firm in their original offerings, and the spice profile becomes less. Sigh.

Don't get me wrong.

Adapting to the market is vitally important for a business to succeed—except when the business changes so much, it has forgotten why it entered the market in the first place. Take care of your clients. Just don't take care of them so much that you lose your uniqueness as a business. In other words, keep the spice! Please and thank you!

Power Thought
Change is great, but don't lost sight
of your core business.

Day 97:
You Fired That Employee.
So Why Do You Not Feel Better?

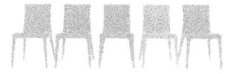

I received a call from a potential client who had recently fired an under-performing employee. This employee was wreaking havoc on the work culture, missing deadlines, throwing others under the bus in meetings and not taking responsibility for their actions. Firing this employee was exactly the right move to make.

"So, why don't I feel better?" he asked.

First, if you ever feel good after you have fired someone, you have lost your humanity and must take a long vacation, effective immediately. In other words, I would worry deeply if you *didn't* feel bad after firing someone. After all, these are people, not cogs in a wheel.

Second, the relationship is over, along with your hopes and dreams for an outstanding performance from that individual. You would not have hired someone that you did not believe could do the job and do it well. When it does not work out as expected, it can feel awful and be perceived as a failure.

Third, you may now be concerned that you have poor judgement and are not skilled at hiring. You begin to think about the time and energy it takes to search for candidates and to wonder if you will ever find the right fit.

There is a way to feel better and restore your confidence.

Ask yourself:

- Did you observe something during the interview process that you knew could have been an issue, but you ignored it?

- Did you give this person an appropriate level of training to be successful in their position?

- Did you give them coaching and council to improve performance with time for course correction?

- Did you let them know, in no uncertain terms, that without improvement they would be fired?

Only through a thorough review process of a poorly performing employee post-employment, from search to departure, can you identify places to improve hiring and retention.

Then, after you debrief, I want you to breathe and cut yourself some slack. Everyone has a bad hire occasionally. You did the best you could in that moment. You will do better next time. I believe in you!

Power Thought

One bad hire doesn't disqualify you from being
a great hiring manager.

Day 98:
My Conversation with a Venture Capitalist

About ten years ago, I had a chance to meet with a very successful venture capitalist to discuss my business. I had an idea that someone in the VC world might be a great referral partner for me; great staff increases value in a company.

The kind gentleman whom I connected and scheduled with thought that I had come to make a pitch for money, which I wasn't interested in at the time. To be fair, our agendas weren't in alignment from the beginning.

I walked into his office, and he had a speed chess timer set for 15:00 minutes. He started the timer rolling, and waited for me to begin.

When I was about three minutes into my spiel, he stopped me and said, "Staffing professionals are all the same. They drop the same statistics and do not talk about how to solve the problem of hiring the wrong people." With this statement, he rose. Our interaction was clearly over. I left at six-and-a-half minutes.

Those minutes changed my life.

I realized that my sales pitch was totally wrong, even if my intention at the time was not about raising funds. It occurred to me that focusing on the fear around the issue of hiring did not inspire anyone, from venture capitalist to employer to my client. Everyone knows the hiring process is broken; my repeating that fact helps no one.

Since then, I have changed my pitch completely to *exclude* any fear-based language, and to *include* my story (the bad hiring mistake that made national news) and educational language. I talk about how I can help my potential clients find the right people, so they can grow their businesses and meet their missions.

I am incredibly grateful for the feedback that the VC gave to me. Without that meeting, I wouldn't be where I am today.

Power Thought

Have the right pitch for the right audience.

Day 99:
Do You Prepare Before You Interview a Candidate?

I met with a potential client who is searching for a new Director of Sales. He reports making several "mis-hires" of this particularly key position in his company. He reached out to me to develop a better recruiting and hiring program, as his current method did not appear to be working.

During our discussion, he said, "I just don't know what I am doing wrong."

I replied, "How much time do you take to prepare before you interview someone?"

He looked at me blankly, then said, "Prepare? What do you mean?"

"Let me re-phrase the question," I said. "When you are about to interview a sales person, what preparation do you do before you interview them?"

"Well, I review their resume. Then I interview them."

"How much time does that typically take you?" I asked.

"A few minutes to review the resume, then the actual interview."

"How much money does a good salesperson make for you in a year?"

"A good salesperson will generate $3–4 million in revenue."

To which I responded, "So, you spend a few minutes preparing for a multi-million-dollar investment?"

I was met with silence, followed by a deep sigh of revelation from this employer.

The lesson in this story?

If you want your new employee to be successful in their new position, you must prepare *before* you hire, by setting them up with great training, realistic expectations and a definition of desired job performance. To prepare, remember to create an *ideal candidate list*, a solid *job description*, and an established, *consistent interview process* before you talk to anyone!

Remember these 5 Ps of business: Prior Preparation Prevents Poor Performance. You want the best employee that money can buy. Prepare for them!

Power Thought

Prior preparation will prepare you for success.

Day 100:
Are Your Candidates Ghosting You?

I have had several business owners and hiring managers ask me about why candidates are "ghosting" them for interviews. In case you are not familiar with the term, ghosting means "the practice of ending a personal relationship with someone by suddenly, and without explanation, withdrawing from all communication."

Apparently, candidates are ghosting potential employers with increased frequency. The job seeker applies for a job and when the company calls them for an interview, the candidate either never responds or schedules the interview and then never shows up. Several employers that I have discussed this issue with are really upset, and rightly so, especially when the candidate schedules and does not show up for interviews.

If you are encountering this issue, here are a few suggestions:

1. Most importantly, take a big deep breath. If a candidate does not up for an interview, you now have at least thirty minutes to get something else done that you may not have had time to accomplish in your day.

2. The candidate did you a huge favor by not attending the interview. No call/no show behavior would have most likely appeared in their job performance if they had made it through the hiring process and began working for you. Be grateful; they just made your job easier by not having to fire them later.

3. I am seeing ghosting from all levels of candidates, from entry level to senior level, and in all industries. It is not just you and your organization this is happening to, so do not take it personally.

4. Remember that employers are the ones that started ghosting when we quit responding to *all* candidate inquiries. A simple "Thanks but no thanks." is all recruits want when they apply and are not chosen. As hiring professionals, it is hard to justify being too upset when non-responsiveness to candidates has become common place.

5. Turn the opportunity into a positive learning experience. Remember that candidates also deserve your best customer service. Return messages, calls and emails in a timely fashion. Be courteous and do what you say you are going to do when you set expectations with your potential hires.

You cannot eliminate all ghosting from candidates, but you can do your part to create a great place to work. That means be a great "host" and quit being a "ghost."

Power Thought

Be the example you want to see from others.

Day 101:
Do You Know What Recruiting is *Not?*

I received a call from a potential client who said, "I need help recruiting. Do you do that?"

I told him that I did provide recruiting services, then asked, "What makes you think that you need help with recruiting?"

He said, "I can't find the right people."

"Have you posted a job advertisement online?"

Yes, he had.

I asked, "Are you getting applicants?"

Yes, he was getting applicants.

"Then you do not need help recruiting," I told him. "You need help interviewing."

■　■　■　■　■

Most business leaders are confused about what recruiting *does* for their hiring process, and what it *does not* do. Recruiting is asking people to apply for a job. Interviewing is the screening process to finding someone to work for you. Hiring is the yes or no question that you ask yourself, before making a job offer. Recruiting is simply getting the applicants. That's it. No more. No less.

So let us be clear on what recruiting does *not* do:

- Recruiting doesn't help you select the right candidate. *Interviewing* does that.

- Recruiting doesn't help you figure out what you want. Creating an *Ideal Candidate Profile* and accurate *job description* does that.

- Recruiting doesn't ensure that you will be successful in your hiring efforts. An *effective hiring process* does that.

The terminology around hiring employees is jargon-based, confusing and not very helpful. Educate yourself about the entire hiring process, before beginning your search.

Happy recruiting! (And interviewing and hiring!)

Power Thought

Educate yourself before interviewing will help
you have a clear understanding of what you need.

MOVING FORWARD

Every time I fill a position, I am on a complete high ... for about 6 hours. Then, I am deeply depressed because I won't be working with that client anymore. That search is over, and it won't ever be the same again. AND ... I am also filled with a sense of pride. We did it. We fought through the roadblocks, the myths, the impatience and lack of faith, and our candidate showed up. It really is nothing short of miraculous!

I sure hope you feel this way about this book being over!

When I follow up with my clients after we have hired someone together, the comments are always the same: "Beth, this process WORKS!" "I had no idea how great it could be to have the right person in this seat!" "I am in love with my work again, because I have the right team in place!"

If I could only teach you ONE thing: it is to be patient. There is this insane pressure to fill a position with anyone when you have an empty seat, but it just never feels right.

So, hold out. Stay true to your Ideal List and keep moving forward.

You can do this. I have your back.

ACKNOWLEDGEMENTS

My People. My Purpose. My Gratitude.

A-list Interviews Clients: Bless every one of you for taking the leap of faith to work with me. I am a lucky girl!

AuthorSource: Simon Presland and Mike Owens. Another excellent collaboration! Thank you both for your hard work!

Beth Boen: For your twice a year calls that keep us apprised of our lives. I love those calls!

Beth Steinmetz: Who knew that a Mommy and Me class 23 years ago would lead to this? Thank you for letting me be a pseudo member of your family!

Focus Marketing & PR: Niki Lopez and Brooke Kuhn: Thank you for getting me to where I need to go! Our collaboration is so inspiring!

Kristin Lukela: I am in such a transformed place now, and I couldn't have done it without your patience and support. Love, Butch.

Lisa Harris: We keep getting better and better. I am so grateful to you!

Mandi Hogan: No matter where we are, we always come back to our friendship. Here is to our next 30 years. Love you!

Mary Hegy: Our friendship is truly full of *happy* hours. Text me when you get home!

Melissa Nance: Girl! We have been through it! Overthinkers unite!

Meryem Ersoz: Book Club enhanced! I so appreciate our dedication to each other's goals.

Mikki Williams: Mentor Extraordinaire. Kizmet!

My babies that I didn't give birth to: A.J. Sellers, Ash Lloyd, Courtney Peterson, Dominique Kennedy, Kenna Mavel, Kelli McDermott, Quinn Riesch, and Tater Tot. My heart is full, my soul is blessed by all of you. Reach for the stars, my babies!

Phil Koffler: Thank you for leading me through pain to ultimate health.

Randy Smith: Our relationship as parents and co-workers is so important to me. Thank you for your hard work and dedication in both!

Tonya Auville: My hair looks so good! Thank you for your brilliance and our deep conversations.

Triple D: Laura Hein and Tina Ramey: Through thick and thin … it is not for the "faint" of heart. ☺

Vistage: Every time I leave a meeting, I think, That was such a great use of my time! Thank you for the tough love and continued support!

www.ingramcontent.com/pod-product-compliance
Lightning Source LLC
Chambersburg PA
CBHW040925210326
41597CB00030B/5177